D0831679

CHINA SMART

CHINA SMART

● ●

**What You *DON'T* Know,
What You *NEED* to Know**

A Past & Present Guide to

History, Culture, Society, Language

Larry Herzberg

Stone Bridge Press • *Berkeley, California*

Published by
Stone Bridge Press
P. O. Box 8208, Berkeley, CA 94707
tel 510-524-8732 • sbp@stonebridge.com • www.stonebridge.com

The film *The China Threat: Perception versus Reality* by Larry and Qin Herzberg has been shared with hundreds of educational institutions. If you work for a school in the U.S. and would like a complimentary copy, contact the author at herz@calvin.edu and request one. DVD copies are also available for purchase from the Calvin College Bookstore at Calvin College, Grand Rapids, MI.

Cover design by Linda Ronan.

Printed in the United States of America.

2021 2022 2021 2020 2019   9 8 7 6 5 4 3 2 1

p-ISBN: 978-1-61172-050-1
e-ISBN: 978-1-61172-935-1

Contents

China's Society, Culture, and Language

China Today

Note to the Reader

China is the world's most populous nation and has now become the number two economy in the world. Yet most people in the United States (and the rest of the Western world) know far too little about it. As a professor of Chinese language and culture over the past four decades, I have felt it increasingly important to point out many of the notable things about China, both in the past and in the present, that are generally an untold story. I have also made it my mission to correct many of the misconceptions that a great majority of Americans have about a country the U.S. is involved with more than ever before.

In this book I have attempted to introduce to a general audience some of the most significant and fascinating aspects of both ancient and contemporary China. Included are fifty-nine articles divided into three major sections: China's Past; Chinese Society, Culture, and Language; and China Today.

In the section on China's past are short commentaries about everything from the history of the Great Wall and the origin of silk, porcelain, and tea to the story of the only female emperor as well as the history of Chinese migration to the U.S. The section on Chinese society, culture, and language contains short essays about, for example, the nature of the spoken and written languages, the various ethnic groups within China, the major holidays, and superstitions regarding numbers. The final section on China today covers topics as diverse as the recent economic miracle, pollution, gender inequality, and China's emerging role on the world stage.

For the most part I have deliberately avoided controversial subjects such as human rights abuses or the perceived economic threat to the U.S. posed by China's rise. Those highly complex issues I did attempt to examine in a 2½-hour documentary that my Chinese wife and I produced in 2012, entitled "The China Threat: Perception versus Reality," which has been shared with hundreds of educational institutions in the U.S. (If you attend or work for a school, see the copyright page of this book for information about obtaining a complimentary copy.)

What I offer here instead is a glimpse into some of the defining aspects of China, both historically and in today's world. I have tried to make it interesting and entertaining while also providing some substantial educational value. This book was written for students of the Chinese language and culture and also for those traveling to China for business or pleasure who wish to learn more about the country they will be visiting. Above all, it is for anyone who aspires to deepen their knowledge of a country so very important in the times in which we live. I hope you will discover how much there is about China that is absolutely intriguing and worth learning about.

Larry Herzberg
Professor of Chinese
Director of Asian Studies
Calvin College
Grand Rapids, Michigan

China's Past

1

● ●

Origin of the Word "China"

The word we use in English to describe the world's most populous country actually bears no resemblance to the term the "Chinese" themselves use.

There are various scholarly theories regarding the origin of the word "China." The traditional theory most popularly accepted today was proposed in the 17th century by Martino Martini, an Italian Jesuit missionary, cartographer, and historian who spent much of his life in China. Martini posited that "China" is derived from "Qin" (秦, pronounced "chin"), the name of the westernmost of the Chinese kingdoms during the Zhou dynasty and that of the succeeding Qin dynasty (221–206 BC), under which the various kingdoms were first united.

However, some scholars now believe that the word "China" is actually derived from "Cin," a Persian name for China popularized in Europe by Marco Polo. The first recorded use in English dates from 1555. In early usage, "china" as a term for porcelain was spelled differently from the name of the country, the two words being derived from separate Persian words. Both these words came from the Sanskrit word "Cīna," used as a name for China as early as AD 150. In the Hindu scriptures *Mahābhārata* (5th century BC) and *Manusmṛti* (Laws of Manu; 2nd century BC), the Sanskrit word "Cīna" is used to refer to a country located in the Tibeto-Burman borderlands east of India.

Even if the Jesuit Father Martini had been correct about the word "China" deriving from the name of the first Chinese dynasty, the Chinese people would never have called their country by that name in subsequent centuries. The Qin dynasty was by far the briefest of all Chinese dynasties. It lasted a mere fifteen years, ending only four years after the death of the First Emperor. During his eleven-year reign the first Qin Emperor did have some impressive accomplishments. He undertook gigantic projects, including ordering the building and unifying of various sections of what we now call the Great Wall of China to protect his new country from invasion by the "barbarians" to the north. He created a massive national road system. He also standardized weights and measures and even wheel ruts across all the kingdoms he administered. The Chinese writing system was also standardized for the newly unified country.

Most of this came at the expense of a great many lives. The building of the Great Wall and the national road system was only made possible through the conscripted labor of hundreds of thousands of peasants. These unfortunate men were often taken hundreds of miles from their villages to work many hard years on the frontiers. A large percentage of them never returned to their families but died in these forced-labor projects.

In order to avoid having antigovernment scholars compare his reign with the past, the Qin Emperor ordered most existing books be burned. The only exceptions were those on astrology, divination, medicine, and agriculture, as well as those that related the history of the Kingdom of Qin. The burning of so many books from the past also furthered the ongoing reformation of the writing system by removing examples of variant forms of Chinese characters. Most infamous of all was that this first of the world's book-burning dictators had nearly five hundred scholars buried alive for illicitly owning such classic works as the *Book of Songs* and the *Classic of History*.

Given the cruelty as well as the short-lived nature of this first dynasty, the people we call "Chinese" in later centuries never wanted to be known as the "Qin people" or have their country called the "Kingdom of Qin." Four years after the death of the Qin Emperor, the rebel Liu Bang overthrew the Qin to establish the Han dynasty. This dynasty lasted for more than four centuries, from 206 BC to 220 AD.

It was the first of several golden ages of this newly unified empire. Under Han rule, China greatly expanded its territory and power, conquering what is today northern Korea and northern Vietnam. The "Silk Road" was established to provide a trade route with Rome, the other great civilization of the time. The civil service examination system was created to select officials, based largely on the teachings of Confucius. Under Han rule, the country produced important works of history, medicine, philosophy, poetry, and politics. Artists produced glazed pottery, large stone carvings. bronze vessels, and exquisite lacquer work. Silk was woven in rich colors and creative patterns to become a major industry and a source of export trade. And it was during the Han dynasty that China invented paper, sundials, and a seismograph.

In recognition of China's achievements during this period, the Chinese people for several millennia have referred to themselves as the Han people. The pictographs that form their writing system are called "Han characters" ("Hànzì"), pronounced by the Japanese as *kanji*. And the spoken language is referred to in mainland China today as the "Han language" ("Hànyǔ"). Since 1911, when the last imperial dynasty was overthrown, the "Chinese" have referred to their country as 中国 ("Zhōngguó," "the Middle Kingdom") and call themselves 中国人 ("Zhōngguó rén," "people of the Middle Kingdom"). The term "Zhōngguó" was in use even before the Qin dynasty and was adopted by subsequent Chinese rulers to reflect their belief that their country was the center of civilization for all the countries that surrounded it.

Indeed, there is some validity to the Chinese view of themselves. Both Japan and Korea adopted Chinese characters for their writing systems. More than half of all the words in the spoken Japanese and Korean languages have Chinese roots. China also gave Japan and Korea, as well as Vietnam, their traditional architecture, Buddhism, Confucian philosophy, rice cultivation, the use of chopsticks for eating, and much more.

If for the last century the Chinese have referred to their country as "Zhōngguó" and call themselves "Zhōngguó rén," the official name of both the People's Republic of China and the Republic of China (Taiwan) use the term 中华 ("Zhōnghuá," "Middle Hua People"). "Hua" is the name in ancient China used to distinguish the cultured "Chinese" people from the barbarians living around them. The official name of the PRC (i.e., mainland China) is 中华人民共和国 ("Zhōnghuá Rénmín Gònghéguó," "Middle Hua People's Republic"), while Taiwan calls itself merely 中华民国 ("Zhōnghuá Mínguó," "Middle Hua Republic").

In any case, neither "Zhōngguó" nor "Zhōnghuá," nor the term "Han," has anything at all to do with the English terms "China" and "Chinese," just as "Germany" has no connection with the term the people of that country use for their nation, namely "Deutschland."

2

● ●

The Great Wall

To foreigners, the Great Wall is the best known and most celebrated structure in China. It seems to us, and to the Chinese as well, a symbol of the greatness of ancient China. No trip to China seems complete without a visit to "The Wall."

This manmade wonder is truly an incredible achievement. Without modern construction equipment, the Chinese were able to build a wall that stretches from east to west across approximately 1,000 miles of often rugged and inhospitable terrain, with nearly 4,000 miles of walled structures. When Richard Nixon stood on the Wall in 1972, during his trip to restore U.S. relations with China, he famously declared, "This is a Great Wall and it had to be built by a great people."

And yet many myths persist about the Wall, as Julia Lovell points out in her insightful book, *The Great Wall: China Against the World.*

Myth #1 is that it is one long, continuous structure that has existed in its present form ever since the time of the First Emperor in the 3rd century BC. The first mention of the Wall in the Chinese historical record is in the 1st century BC and refers to the walls built in the two previous centuries, including those by the Qin Emperor, which often joined already existing fortifications constructed by former Chinese states when China was divided.

The Wall, incidentally, has never been called the "Great Wall" by the Chinese but rather "the Long Wall." The English

term is certainly more grandiose, but inaccurate. The "Long Wall" is rarely mentioned in Chinese sources between the end of the Han dynasty in 220 AD and the beginning of the Ming dynasty in 1368. That is because so much of it fell into disrepair in the intervening millennium. Much of the Wall as we know it today is the result of building during the Ming dynasty in the 14th through the 17th centuries. In recent centuries the greatest part of the Wall has crumbled in many places and is hardly visible. The places tourists visit today are reconstructions done in the past three decades under the Chinese Communist government.

Myth #2 about the Great Wall is that it clearly marked the border between the Chinese on one side and the barbarians to the north on the other. It is viewed as expressing the Chinese belief that they were culturally superior to all other peoples and therefore wanted to keep all foreigners out. This ignores the fact that during the Han dynasty (206 BC–AD 220) and the Tang dynasty (AD 618–907) in particular, China welcomed in

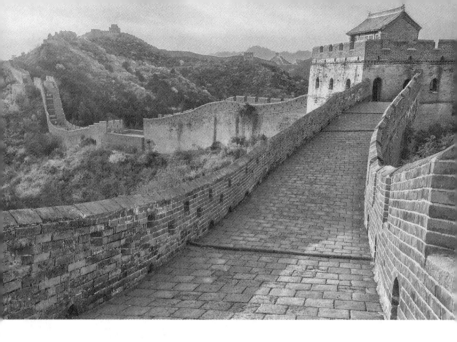

people from many cultures to the west, including Jews and Muslims. For much of Chinese history, the country was ruled by emperors who loved and emulated many aspects of the nomad cultures to the north, or who themselves came from the steppes to the north. The latter includes the Mongol rulers, who controlled China from 1260 to 1368 AD and the Manchus, who ruled from 1644 to 1911.

Myth #3 is that the Wall was a symbol of the power and prestige of ancient China. It was more commonly used as a strategy for defense on the frontier borders of the country. The Wall was seen as the last resort for dealing with the barbarians when all else, including trade, diplomacy, and military expeditions, had failed. The Wall is better seen as a symbol of the weakness and failure of the Chinese emperors.

The cost of trying to maintain this sprawling defensive structure bankrupted many of China's weaker rulers and led to the overthrow of their dynasties. To the common people in ancient China, the Wall represented the misery of conscripted labor, with hundreds of thousands of young men forced from their villages to either build or guard this frontier barrier. Most never returned and the bones of a great many of them were buried next to and beneath it. There are famous poems by Tang-dynasty poets like Du Fu that express the sorrow of the peasants dragged away from their homes and that of their wives left to mourn.

The Great Wall also proved little protection from marauding barbarians intent on conquering China. When the Mongol hordes under Genghis Khan conquered China in the 13th century AD, they had little problem circumventing this supposedly impregnable barrier. So it was, too, with the Manchus from the northeast, when they invaded China in the early 17th century. The invading armies either made detours around the defenses to find gaps or weak spots in the Wall, or they simply bribed the Chinese officials assigned to guard the lonely outposts to let them through.

Myth #4 is that the Great Wall was built for purely defensive reasons, to protect the peaceful Chinese peasants in the border areas from invasions by marauding barbarians. In actuality, from even well before the Qin Emperor, the rulers of various Chinese states built walls far out into the steppes of Mongolia to the north as well as into the deserts of northwest China, hundreds of miles from any arable land. The purpose was originally more to expand the territory under Chinese control and to protect trade routes to the West than it was to protect the "civilized" Chinese from the "uncivilized barbarians."

The last myth about the Wall, shared until recently by the Chinese as well as by foreigners, is that the Great Wall is the only manmade structure that can be seen from the moon, as reported by the U.S. media. Actually, until China launched its first manned space flight in 2003, textbooks in China declared that the Wall was one of two man-made structures visible from the moon. The other was a sea embankment in the

Netherlands. When the astronaut of the 2003 voyage, Yang Liwei, returned to Earth, he announced with great embarrassment that he wasn't able to see the slightest evidence of the Great Wall from the moon. Only then did the Ministry of Education in China instruct elementary school teachers to stop trumpeting to students that their symbol of national pride could be viewed from outer space.

Nevertheless, the Great Wall is evidence of the immense power and scope of the Chinese empire in past centuries, governed by rulers who were able to undertake such a monumental building project over hundreds of years.

3

The Imperial Examination System

Well over a thousand years before government officials in Europe or Japan were chosen on the basis of ability and knowledge and not simply by the class into which they were born, Chinese officials at all levels of government were appointed by means of an elaborate civil service examination system. It was this examination system that later inspired the British civil service exams that began in the mid-19th century, on which a few decades later the U.S. then modeled some its own governmental exams.

Imperial exams in China were held as early as the Han dynasty, around two thousand years ago, but the system only became widely used as the major path to office in the

8th century, in the middle period of the Tang dynasty, and remained in use until it was abolished in 1905. The exams were based on knowledge of the canon of five classic Confucian books as well as the ability to write in an elegant literary style. Knowledge of a shared common culture helped to unify the Chinese empire, and creating the ideal of advancement by merit helped give legitimacy to imperial rule. However, it also created obvious problems, as the system failed to test or reward technical and practical expertise.

One notable result of reliance on an examination system was the shift in ruling power from a military aristocracy to an elite class of scholar-officials who headed the bureaucracy. By the Song dynasty in the 10th and 11th centuries, the system had been standardized and developed into a three-tiered progressive set of tests from local to provincial to national exams. In Europe all government positions would continue to be given only to the members of the aristocracy, based solely on birth, for many centuries to come. Medieval China was thus far ahead of its time in pioneering the idea of basing positions in the ruling class almost entirely on education and not on social class.

Rigid quotas restricted the number of successful candidates at each level. For example, only three hundred students could pass the examinations at the national level. Students often took the examinations several times before earning a degree. The entry-level exams were offered annually and were open to any educated men from their teen years on; successful candidates were eligible for positions such as district magistrate. The provincial exams were held every three years in the capital cities of each province; successful candidates were eligible for the highest government offices in each province. The national exams to choose officials at the national level were also held every three years in the nation's capital. Finally there were the palace exams to choose the prime minister and other top advisers to the imperial court; these were often supervised by the emperor himself.

For each of the exams candidates were only allowed to bring a very few items to the exam locations, namely a water pitcher, a chamber pot, bedding, food (which he had to prepare himself), ink and brushes, and an inkstone. Guards were posted to verify each student's identity and to search for any hidden printed materials. From the 14th through the early 20th centuries each examination candidate spent three days and two nights in a tiny room with a makeshift bed, desk, and bench, writing literary compositions with eight distinct sections. No outside communication or any other interruptions were allowed during that three-day period.

Intense pressure to succeed made cheating and corruption all too common, in spite of the strenuous efforts to prevent them. To discourage any favoritism that might occur if an examiner recognized a particular student's calligraphy, each exam handed in was recopied by an official copyist. Exact quotes from the classic Confucian and neo-Confucian texts were required. Misquoting even one character or writing it in the wrong form meant failure, so candidates went to great lengths to bring hidden copies of these texts with them, sometimes written on their undergarments.

Critics complained that the system stifled creativity and created officials who dared not defy authority. But it did help promote cultural unity. Wealthy families, especially from the merchant class, could help their sons achieve official posts by paying to educate them or even by purchasing degrees.

It was even possible, although extremely difficult, for a peasant boy to educate himself and pass the exams needed to reach high office. A few notable cases in Chinese history helped keep the notion alive that any boy could reach officialdom. However, by the 19th century critics blamed the imperial system, and by extension its examinations, for

China's lack of technical knowledge and its defeat by foreign powers.

Despite the shortcomings of the Chinese examination system, its influence spread to neighboring Asian countries such as Korea and Vietnam. It was introduced to the Western world in written reports by European missionaries and diplomats, which inspired the British East India Company in the 19th century to adopt a similar exam system for selecting its employees. Observing the success of that company's hiring policy, the British government adopted a similar testing system for screening civil servants in 1855. Other European nations, such as France and Germany, followed Britain's example. Modeled on these European exam systems, the U.S created its own testing program for certain government jobs after 1883. Candidates for posts in the U.S. Foreign Service are most likely unaware that the exams they are given were inspired by the Chinese imperial exams of a great many centuries ago.

4

● ●

Two Bloody Civil Wars

Two of the bloodiest military conflicts in human history occurred in China, and yet few people in the West have ever heard of them.

The An Lushan Rebellion
The An Lushan Rebellion occurred during the Tang

dynasty, when China was arguably the most powerful empire in the world, and lasted from December of 755 until February of 763. General An Lushan hungered for power and launched a rebellion against an emperor he claimed was decadent and weak. He declared himself emperor in the northern part of the country and established the Yan dynasty. The rebellion was continued by his son and lasted through the reigns of three Tang emperors before it was finally put down. This rebellion, unknown in the West except to students of Chinese history, resulted in a tremendous loss of life and almost unparalleled large-scale destruction.

An Lushan was a general of unknown parentage who yet managed to gain favor with the emperor. He was made commander of a huge area in the north of the empire and oversaw garrisons with over 150,000 men. Eventually he took advantage of popular unrest caused by the extravagant lifestyle of the court; this coincided with another rebellion that had taken troops away from the palace, as well as a series of natural disasters.

General An Lushan and his rebel forces in 756 managed to capture the empire's capital Chang'an, overrunning one of the largest and most prosperous cities in the world at the time. Chang'an's greater metropolitan area was estimated to have a population of as many as one million people when it was conquered. The majority of the population fled the city as the rebels approached, and the city was thoroughly looted.

The emperor finally regained control, in large part because of the internal disputes among the rebel forces. An Lushan became extremely paranoid and was killed by his son in 757. That son was then assassinated by one of his generals, who had been a childhood friend of An Lushan and a devoted follower. But that general was subsequently killed by his son. Although imperial forces finally restored order eight years after the rebellion broke out, the Tang dynasty was greatly weakened both financially and in terms of the amount of territory it controlled.

The An Lushan Rebellion resulted in the death of millions of people, greatly reducing the population of the empire. Death came not just from war and its collateral damage among civilians, but also due to the disruption of the economy. In the northern half of the country mass starvation and disease killed off millions. Since census figures of the time are not considered reliable by historians, estimates are anywhere from thirteen million deaths to as many as thirty-six million. The latter figure means that around two-thirds of the empire's population perished in those years, which would have amounted to around one-sixth of the world's population at that time. Even if the much lower figure of thirteen million dead is more accurate, it means a loss of approximately 5% of the population of the entire world in the 8th century in only a decade.

The Taiping Rebellion

Another devastating civil war in China occurred more than a thousand years later. It began on January 1 of 1851 and lasted until the summer of 1864, just a year before the Civil War in the U.S. ended. This civil war in China, known as the Taiping Rebellion, far exceeded the American Civil War in loss of life, yet is hardly known in the West.

The rebellion began in Guangxi Province in the far south of China, far from Beijing, when local officials began a campaign of religious persecution of a Christian millenarian sect that called itself the "God Worshiping Society." The sect was led by a man named Hong Xiuquan, a failed candidate in the civil service examinations. Hong was influenced by Christian teachings and, after a series of visions, declared himself to be the younger brother of Jesus Christ destined to reform China. The goal of the sect was to convert the Chinese people to its brand of Christianity, overthrow the Qing government controlled by the foreign Manchus since their invasion of China in the 17th century, and totally transform Chinese society to make it more egalitarian. They sought to create the 太平天国 (Tàipíng Tiānguó), the "Heavenly Kingdom of Universal Peace," with Hong as the Heavenly King. Their espoused ideal of sharing all property in common attracted a great many poor peasants who suffered from extremely high taxes and who had no love for the Manchus who ruled China.

War broke out on January 1, 1851, when forces of the Qing army attacked the God Worshiping Society in the town of Jintian in Guangxi Province. To escape the government's army, Hong eventually led his Taiping followers on a long march that ended in March 1853 when he and his forces managed to capture the major southern city of Nanjing, which Hong declared to be the capital of his Heavenly Kingdom. By this time Hong's army had grown from a ragtag group of several thousand to more than a million soldiers, separated into male and female divisions, who were highly disciplined and fanatic in their devotion to the cause.

The version of Christianity espoused by Hong and his followers emphasized the Old Testament ideals of worship and obedience, rather than the New Testament ideals of love and forgiveness. Nevertheless, the Taiping sect promoted the equality of the sexes. Prostitution, adultery, foot-binding, and slavery were prohibited. So, too, were tobacco and opium, alcohol, and gambling.

For the next decade the Taiping forces occupied a large section of the mid- and lower Yangtse River valley, some of the wealthiest and most productive land in the empire, from where they continued to battle government forces. The Taiping rebels came close to capturing the Qing capital of Beijing in May 1853 and were successful in taking over large parts of three provinces, including Jiangxi, Anhui, and Hubei. This meant that they controlled a population of nearly thirty million people. The imperial troops were unable for the most part to stop the advancing rebel army and ended up focusing their efforts on an extremely protracted siege of the Taiping capital of Nanjing.

After fourteen years of bloody fighting, an ailing Hong Xiuquan committed suicide in June 1864. His capital city of Nanjing fell to government forces only a month later, effectively ending the rebellion. Having been promised eternal life in Heaven for their devotion to the cause, the Taiping followers astonished the victorious Qing general when nearly a hundred thousand of them chose death over capture when Nanjing was overrun by government troops.

This prolonged military conflict affected nearly every province of China and became the most large-scale war of the 19th century and the bloodiest civil war in human history. While the total number of deaths can never be known, at least twenty million people lost their lives, with millions more having to flee their homes.

In the parts of China under Taiping rule the Chinese language was simplified, and equality between men and women was decreed. All property was to be held in common, and there was a plan for equal distribution of the land. Some of the leaders of the movement, influenced by the West, even proposed creating a democracy and promoting the establishment of certain industries. After the long and devastating war that the Qing government had to wage to squelch the rebellion, it was so weakened that it was unable to ever fully regain control of the country. The Chinese Communist Party in the 20th century hailed the Taiping Rebellion as the origin of their revolution and of many of their ideals.

5

Empress Wu: China's Queen Elizabeth I?

It may surprise you to learn that China has had as many as three women rulers in past centuries. Only one, however, established herself as the recognized monarch and is credited with major accomplishments. That exceptional woman is Wu Zetian, who lived from 624 to 705. She was arguably China's equivalent to England's Queen Elizabeth I, who lived a thousand years later. Empress Wu first ruled China unofficially as the consort of the emperor, then as the empress dowager, and finally officially as emperor from 684 until shortly before her death in 705. Her reign in essence lasted a half century.

Wu Zetian's father was quite successful in the business of forestry, and she grew up in great comfort. The family did not belong to the aristocracy, although her father ingratiated himself with the Tang-dynasty emperor and was eventually appointed to high posts in the government. He saw to it that his daughter received an excellent education, which was highly unusual for women of that day. When Wu Zetian was merely fourteen years old she was given to the emperor as one of his many concubines. Because she was one of the few concubines who was educated, she was given a position as a scribe and continued her education. But she was not particularly favored by the emperor, Taizong.

When Emperor Taizong died in 649, his youngest son, Li Zhi, succeeded him and, unlike his father, had sexual relations with Wu Zetian, even while his father was still alive.

However, since Wu Zetian had failed to give Emperor Taizong any children, by custom she was sent to live out her days as a nun in a Buddhist convent. Breaking with all convention, after Emperor Taizong's death Li Zhi visited Wu Zetian in the convent. Finding she had grown to be a great beauty as well as a woman of great intelligence, he brought her back to his palace as his concubine, where she became the empress consort in 655. When the emperor suffered a debilitating stroke in 660, Wu Zetian took over the administration of the court, in effect exercising actual control of the government.

After the death of her husband, Wu Zetian became the empress dowager. She poisoned the crown prince and exiled other princes with a claim to the throne, and then had her third son, Li Zhe, declared the heir apparent. She had convinced her husband before his death to state in his will that should Li Zhe as a youth ascend to the throne, she as his mother would be consulted in all major affairs, whether civil or military.

When her son who had become emperor failed to obey her wishes, she quickly had him deposed and replaced him with her youngest son, whom she made a virtual prisoner in the palace while she became the visible ruler. Finally in 690 her son officially yielded the throne to her, and she had herself declared the emperor. This was the first and only time China ever had a woman as the supreme ruler in name as well as in fact.

In the early part of her reign, Empress Wu employed a kind of secret police to ensure her hold on power. She eliminated many of her potential rivals who might threaten her hold on power by either sending her agents to execute them or by ordering them to commit suicide.

As time went on she proved herself a most able ruler who wisely chose very capable officials to help her govern the empire. During her reign her army managed to significantly expand the Chinese empire far beyond its former borders in Central Asia. Her forces were even able to annex Korea for the first time in Chinese history. She instituted a system of soldier-farmer colonies that provided her with local militia and laborers, enabling her to maintain her army at far less expense than had previously been possible.

Domestically Wu Zetian gained popular support by enacting policies that helped the common people. She benefited from the fact that she came to power during a time of relative peace and prosperity, with the economy strong and living standards on the rise. Empress Wu ensured that the peasants could continue to farm their own land, making sure that land was allocated fairly based on regularly updated census figures. She also ordered a number of acts that gave relief to the poorer elements of society. At a time when Buddhism had gained a huge following, Empress Wu further ingratiated herself with the common people by ordering the building of a great many Buddhist temples and pagodas, including the famous Wild Goose Pagoda.

Wu Zetian continued to employ the imperial examination system to recruit officials on every level, but she greatly increased the number of eligible applicants by allowing for the first time commoners and lesser gentry to take the exams and thus rise in social position. She also put an end to many abuses in both the government and the military.

Although later Chinese Confucian historians vilified her as a ruthless tyrant, finding the idea of a woman emperor repugnant, recent historians in both China and the West have recognized her as a highly capable ruler who should be credited with several major accomplishments during her fairly long reign.

6

● ●

Hua Mulan

Probably no legendary Chinese woman is as celebrated throughout Chinese history as the woman warrior Hua Mulan. And thanks to the Disney movie of 1998, *Mulan*, she is now also known to millions throughout the world. But how did this legend originate, and how much truth is there in the tale of her courage and heroism?

The first mention of this woman warrior is in the *Ballad of Mulan* from the *Musical Records of Old and New* written in the 6th century. However, the earliest remaining copy of the ballad is in an anthology from five centuries later. In less than four hundred characters it tells the story of a brave young woman who in the 5th or 6th century takes the place of her old father to fight for twelve years to keep the kingdom safe from barbarian invasion. She wins great acclaim but refuses any reward except to be allowed to return to her home when the battles are over.

Her story in the original poem is as follows: Mulan sits weaving when she learns that one man from every family in the kingdom has been summoned to serve in the army to defend China from barbarian invaders. Her father is too old and weak to serve, and her younger brother is only a child. Mulan therefore bravely decides to go in place of her father and, with her parents' blessing, goes off to war. She has been well trained in fighting, having received instruction in the martial arts, swordsmanship, and archery. Mulan fights with the army for twelve years, and they eventually vanquish the invaders.

When the army returns and Mulan is offered an official position as a reward for her service, she turns it down and only asks for a strong horse to carry her back home, where she returns to a warm welcome by her family. Only when Mulan resumes wearing the clothing appropriate for her sex do her fellow soldiers realize to their amazement that their companion in all those years of battle was a woman.

Hua Mulan has to be considered more a legend than a historical person. After all, her name does not appear in *Exemplary Women*, which contains the biographies of famous women during the 5th and 6th centuries when Mulan was said to have lived.

In the 16th century the Ming writer Xu Wei dramatized Mulan's story in a play entitled *The Heroine, Mulan, Goes to Fight in Place of Her Father*. And in the 17th century the story was retold in a historical novel penned by the writer Chu Renhou. These authors changed many of the details, but through its various retellings the legend of Hua Mulan has remained one of the most popular Chinese folk tales to this day.

Mulan's name means "magnolia" in Chinese. Her family name differs according to each telling of the story, but the most popular in recent times is "Hua" or "Flower," as in the Ming play, partly because of its poetic connotations.

The story of Hua Mulan has been immortalized in as many as eight films, from the 1927 silent film *Hua Mulan Joins the Army* to the Disney animated film of 1998. A live-action adaption has also been proposed, with a planned release in 2020. There have also been many TV shows that tell her story, from Hong Kong in 1998, Taiwan in 1999, China in 2012, and then again in a CCTV (China Central Television) production in 2013 with forty-nine episodes, as well as in several seasons of the American TV series *Once Upon a Time* in 2012 and 2013. Mulan's story has also been told in several fairly recent English-language books. Maxine Hong Kingston's retelling of Mulan's story in her well-known book *The Woman Warrior* made her tale popular in the West and was possibly the inspiration for Disney's animated film adaptation.

7

Foot-binding

Many in the West have heard that for many centuries in ancient China it was a common custom to bind women's feet. But few Westerners know how and why this custom started, nor are they aware of how it finally came to an end.

Foot-binding involved applying tight binding to the feet of young girls between the ages of four and nine to reshape their feet to make them smaller and, it was thought, more delicate. The toes on each foot were curled under, then pressed downward with great force and squeezed into the sole of the foot until the toes broke.

The custom of foot-binding actually began fairly late in Chinese history, in the 11th or 12th century AD. It was not practiced in the age of Confucius or Lao Zi, nor was it known during the "golden ages" of the Han dynasty (206 BC–AD 220) or the Tang dynasty (AD 618–907).

While we cannot be sure exactly how the practice originated, the generally accepted story is that a favorite concubine of a 10th-century emperor performed a dance for him that required her to balance on her toes. She bound up her feet with white silk to achieve this, and this so entranced the emperor that other court ladies tried to imitate her.

Foot-binding gradually spread to other upper-class women and then over time to the society at large. The earliest references to the custom are in several poems from around 1100.

This cruel practice was not insisted upon by Chinese men, at least not directly. It was instead forced on girls by their mothers in order to make them more attractive to men and ensure a good marriage. The mincing gait produced by foot-binding was considered (by Chinese men) extremely feminine and alluring, and a girl with small "lotus feet" was considered more beautiful than one with larger, naturally shaped feet. It was also a status symbol for a family to have girls and women with bound feet, since that meant they did not need to work in the fields as peasant women had to do. However, foot-binding greatly limited a woman's mobility and resulted in lifelong disabilities for most who underwent this painful procedure.

Most societies throughout human history have been male-dominated, which has resulted in women attempting to attract men by a great variety of different practices, ranging from those that merely caused great discomfort, such as the tight girdles and hoop skirts of 19th-century America, to large lip discs that women in certain African and Amazonian tribes insert in their upper or lower lip. Foot-binding is an extreme example of this attempt to attract a mate.

Foot-binding was not practiced by all Chinese women, by any means. Minority groups like the Hakka in southeastern China did not have this custom. Nor was it the custom of the Manchu people, who conquered China in the 17th century and ruled until 1911. And the majority of peasant families couldn't afford to cripple the feet of their women, whose help they needed to till the fields.

Nevertheless, it is estimated that by the 19th century 40–50% of all Chinese women had bound feet, as did nearly all upper-class Han Chinese women.

Attempts were made to end the practice as early as the 17th century. The Manchu emperor Kangxi tried to ban foot-binding in 1664 but was unsuccessful. In the latter part of the 19th century reform-minded Chinese criticized the practice. But it was only in the early 20th century that foot-binding began to die out as a result of widespread campaigns attacking it. Christian missionaries also preached against what they called a barbaric custom and helped change the opinion of the Chinese elites through their efforts at education, writing pamphlets, and lobbying the court.

In 1912, the government of the newly established Republic of China banned foot-binding but failed to effectively implement the ban. Leading intellectuals at the time declared that foot-binding was symbolic of China's backwardness and needed to be terminated.

By 1949, when the Communist Party assumed power, the practice had been virtually eliminated in most of the country. The Communist government severely criticized the practice, and the last new case of foot-binding was reported in 1957.

However, as recently as 1997 in Beijing, 38% of women aged 80 and older and 18% of women aged 70–79 showed deformities due to foot-binding. Compared to women who had not bound their feet, women who had had their feet bound had substantial disabilities and found it difficult to carry out simple tasks, such as standing up from a chair without assistance. In 1999, the last shoe factory making shoes for foot-bound women closed. In today's China there are only a few very elderly women still alive who show signs of their feet having been subjected to this cruel custom.

8

Zheng He the Sailor

World history textbooks in American schools feature accounts of the voyages of European explorers like Christopher Columbus, Vasco de Gama, and Ferdinand Magellan, who sailed to the ends of the earth in the late 15th and early 16th centuries. But no mention is made of the great Chinese admiral Zheng He, who sailed from the Chinese port city of Nanjing to India, Arabia, and even East Africa several generations before those European explorers and in ships many times larger than theirs.

Zheng He was a Muslim who rose to become the highest-ranking eunuch to serve the Chinese emperor at court. The name Sinbad was very possibly derived from Zheng He's nickname of "San Bao" ("Three Treasures"). He received that appellation because in his white silk cloak he carried a jeweled box that contained his severed penis and testicles, which would accompany him to the next world where he would again become a whole man.

It was the seven epic voyages that Zheng He made between 1405 and 1433 that may have played a small part in inspiring the tales of Sinbad the Sailor and his seven miraculous voyages. The first time the Sinbad stories were included in the tales of *One Thousand and One Nights* wasn't until 1637 in a Turkish collection.

Zheng He's voyages were possible only because China, by the beginning of the Ming dynasty in the mid-14th century, had reached a level of naval technology unsurpassed in the world at that time.

As early as the ninth century, two centuries before the Europeans, the Chinese were using magnetic compasses to navigate. They had printed manuals with star charts and compass bearings several centuries earlier than they became available to European sailors.

By the eighth century, the Chinese were building ships 200 feet long capable of carrying five hundred men, as large as the three ships Columbus used in sailing to the New World eight centuries later.

That the Chinese admiral Zheng He was able to sail to the shores of Africa from China in the early 1400s was remarkable enough, although Chinese merchants had previously visited those same distant ports. The most amazing feature of these voyages was that they were accomplished with hundreds of huge ships and tens of thousands of sailors. Over 60 of the 317 ships on the first voyage were enormous "treasure ships," sailing vessels over 400 hundred feet long, 160 feet wide, with multiple decks, nine masts and twelve sails. They were large enough to carry 2,500 tons of cargo each and were armed with dozens of small cannon. They even featured luxurious staterooms complete with balconies.

Accompanying these ships were hundreds of smaller ships, some filled only with water, others carrying troops or horses or cannon, still others with gifts of silks and brocades, porcelains, lacquerware, tea, and ironworks that would impress leaders of distant civilizations. The likes of these ships had never before been seen in the world, and it would not be until World War I that an armada of this size would be assembled again. Zheng He's "treasure ships" brought back to China sandalwood, hardwood, incense, and tin, as well as exotic African animals such as elephants, lions, and leopards.

On June 29, 1429, Zheng He embarked on his seventh and last voyage, even though the great admiral was fifty-nine years old and in poor health. This last great voyage took three years and stopped at seventeen different ports between India and Kenya. On the way back to China, very possibly in the vicinity of what is now Indonesia, Admiral Zheng He died. He was buried at sea, and his men brought back a braid of his hair and a pair of his shoes to be buried in Nanjing.

Faced with a threat by the Mongols on their northwest border, and the huge financial drain of the expeditions, Ming scholar-officials convinced the Chinese emperor to terminate the extravagant voyages of the Treasure Fleet. An embargo on overseas trade was then maintained by China for the next century, during which time the Western powers' fleets colonized much of the rest of the world.

The conventional view of scholars in both China and the West condemns the Ming government for their short-sightedness in abandoning overseas exploration after Zheng He. But here the Ming dynasty was simply following the Confucian tradition of basing its economic structure on agriculture. The merchant class was viewed with contempt, and trading goods was considered of secondary importance to raising crops. Tying entire populations to their lands proved to be economically practical to an agricultural society and politically desirable for preventing vast social unrest.

Zhu Yuanzhang, the founder of the Ming dynasty, made it a priority to bind his subjects to their farmlands and to instill basic Confucian ethics in all aspects of Ming government and society. Born a poor peasant, Zhu Yuanzhang hated merchants and commerce, closed off ports to foreign traders, and issued edicts forbidding people from leaving the villages where they were registered. Therefore China under Ming rule never developed or endorsed the necessary political, economic, and social structures necessary for successful overseas empires the way that Western countries like Spain, Portugal, England, the Netherlands, or France did.

Adhering to the traditional Confucian notion that China was "superior" to its neighbors, Zheng He's Treasure Ships aimed primarily to impress and awe foreign princes. Gold, silver, porcelain, silk, and other valuables were exchanged, in great quantities, for items worth less than a third of their value. Vast portions of the treasury were spent on Zheng He's voyages, and with little return over the years available funds became depleted. Without a system similar to the European mercantilism that spurred the Dutch and British colonies, the Ming, with their agricultural mindset, were bound to see Zheng He's voyages end in economic disaster. Ming-dynasty China had the power to launch twenty thousand men into the Western seas, but lacked a viable economic structure to maintain its overseas enterprises.

One thing that has always puzzled scholars is why later Chinese rulers sought to destroy any vestiges or records of Zheng He's voyages. Any other country would have been proud to claim such a valiant for its own. It's true that these ventures proved a distraction toward the political agenda of the Ming Emperor, which was the centralization of all power under the Son of Heaven. It has been conjectured that

Emperor Yong Le originally sent Zheng He to the West to seek a prince who had fled the kingdom but who still threatened the throne, as well as to spread the emperor's influence to foreign lands along the way. In this latter regard the voyages at first proved successful, since foreign kings and princes were brought back to Beijing to make their obeisance to the Ming Emperor. Yet, as the voyages continued, the Imperial court may have sensed that Zheng He threatened the sovereignty of the emperor. Just as Copernicus threatened the Catholic Church's teachings with his theories, Zheng He's discoveries of vast new lands beyond the "Middle Kingdom" might have diminished the legitimacy of the ruler. It would be devastating for Ming subjects to learn that the "Middle Kingdom" was only part of a much wider world and that the "Son of Heaven" did not really rule all under Heaven.

Despite attempts to expunge the admiral from history, Chinese monuments and artifacts scattered all around the rim of the Indian Ocean as far as the Kenyan coast provide concrete proof of Zheng He's journeys there. There are also surviving records of several of the voyages in the writings of his Chinese shipmates such as Ma Huan, Gong Zhen, and Fei Xin.

A contemporary Westerner who has revived an interest in Zheng He's voyages is Gavin Menzies. In his best-selling book *1421: The Year China Discovered America*, Menzies argues that China sent out four huge fleets that circumnavigated the globe between March of 1421 and October of 1423 and that one of the fleets reached North America over seventy years before Christopher Columbus. He provides what he believes is compelling proof that the Chinese had the whole world charted by 1423, including the major rivers, so that European explorers set sail with accurate maps showing them the way. In the sequel to that book, *1434: The Year a Magnificent Chinese Fleet Sailed to Italy and Ignited the Renaissance*, Menzies expounds the theory that the arrival of a Chinese fleet in Italy helped spark the Renaissance in Europe. Although these two books are filled with evidence to support Gavin Menzies's theories, the claims they make remain highly controversial.

9

All the Tea in China

Tea is the second most popular beverage in the world, after water. It's impossible to know exactly where the tea plant originated, but most likely tea was first cultivated in southwest China and northern India. Chinese traders may have often traveled through this area and discovered people there chewing on tea leaves for medicinal purposes.

It was not until the Tang dynasty (618–907) that consuming tea as a beverage became so widespread that tea effectively became the national drink. That the Chinese government of the time levied a tax on tea is proof of its popularity.

In the 8th century a Chinese Buddhist monk named Lu Yu composed *Cha Jing* (茶经), the "Classic Book of Tea." In his treatise Lu described the different types of tea, its preparation, its uses, and the benefits of drinking it. He developed the idea of holding a special tea ceremony with a small group of friends and giving it a spiritual element as a way to experience in microcosm the order and harmony of the universe.

Over the following centuries tea came to be more and more romanticized. During the Song dynasty (960–1280) there were a great many poetic references to tea. Chinese culture was beginning to have a huge influence on Korea and Japan, and this included spreading a love of tea to those countries.

It is believed that as early as the 9th century a Japanese Buddhist monk named Saicho had already introduced tea to Japan. While studying in China, Saicho discovered tea and brought back seeds to grow at his monastery. Other monks gradually also began to grow tea, and soon tea was being grown at monasteries in the mountains in many places in Japan. Because these monasteries were so isolated from the rest of the population, tea did not come to be widely consumed in Japan until the 13th century.

The most common way to prepare tea was to grind the young green tea leaves into a fine powder. It wasn't until the Ming dynasty (1368–1644) that tea was prepared by steeping the whole leaves in water, as it is today. Instead of grinding the leaves, they were dried, rolled, and then heated in iron woks to prevent oxidation.

A Chinese monk brought this new rolled tea with him during his travels to Japan in the 17th century. By the 18th century a tea merchant in Kyoto invented a new Japanese method of steaming, drying, and rolling green tea. This process produced a type of tea that eventually became the most popular type of tea in Japan.

Traders, missionaries, and explorers who traveled between Europe and East Asia came to learn of the Chinese and Japanese custom of drinking tea. Marco Polo mentions his discovery of tea in his writings. However, tea drinking did not become popular in the West until the 17th century. It was Dutch merchants who first brought shipments of tea from China and Japan to Europe in the ships of the Dutch East India Company. Tea also started coming into Russia by way of the camel trains that came from China on the famous Silk Road.

The popularity of tea rapidly spread to cities including Amsterdam, Paris, and London, although its rather high

price restricted its enjoyment to royalty and the aristocracy. Tea drinking became an exotic novelty from the East for the wealthy, and it gave them a sense of taking part in an age of exploration and discovery.

The English did not immediately take a fancy to tea. Coffee remained the preferred non-alcoholic drink and was offered in coffee houses frequented mainly by men. But tea slowly became favored by British women, who saw it as a genteel drink. In 1657, the first shop to sell tea in England opened. It sold tea imported by the Dutch and helped bolster the popularity of tea in London's coffee houses and cafes.

As tea grew in popularity in England in the late 1600s, the British East India Trade Company became a major competitor with the Dutch, taking over control of a tea factory in Macao, a Portuguese colony off the coast of southeastern China.

By the early 1700s, the British East India Company

established itself as the dominant trading power in Asia and eventually monopolized the tea trade with China. The company set up trading stations in India, centered in Bombay, Bengal, and Madras.

China remained the primary source of tea for the West until the mid-1800s. In order to discover the secret of growing tea and to end their dependence on Chinese tea, the British sent Robert Fortune, an English botanist, on an undercover mission to China. Disguised as a Chinese merchant he traveled around the country learning about the manner of growing and processing tea. He sent back samples of various teas to England and brought back with him Chinese tea experts who helped the British plant tea in India. The tea industry in India began to flourish, especially after the discovery of a special kind of tea in the Darjeeling region of northern India, and the West's reliance on tea from China came to an end.

Tea first came to America in the mid-1600s by way of the Dutch settlement of New Amsterdam. The colony was captured by England in 1664 and renamed New York, where the tea trade flourished thanks to its popularity among the wealthier colonists, and in particular women. At the same time, the British East India Company persuaded the English Parliament to levy heavy taxes on colonial tea merchants, while allowing the Company to ship directly to the colonists duty-free.

This angered the American colonists, who began to protest that there should be "no taxation without representation." The protests culminated in the Boston Tea Party, as colonists protested England's high taxes by dumping tea from East India Company ships into the harbor. After the American Revolution, Richard Twining and thousands of independent tea merchants worked together to reveal the corrupt practices of the East India Company and put pressure to end their monopoly. By the 1850s American sailing ships had begun importing tea from China. The dominance of the East India Company faded, gradually resulting in the end of the Company in 1874.

During the 19th century, tea drinking became an important part of social life in America as its popularity grew. Iced tea was first introduced at the 1904 World's Fair in St. Louis, Missouri. A tea merchant wanted to hand out free samples of hot tea. However, because of the unusually hot weather during the fair, few people were interested in drinking a hot beverage. To boost his sales, the tea merchant asked a nearby ice cream vendor for some ice, which he dumped into the brewed tea, and it was a hit. Iced tea now accounts for around 80% of all tea sales in the U.S.

There are six basic categories of tea, including black tea, dark tea, oolong tea, green tea, white tea, and puer tea, with hundreds of sub-varieties. While black tea is the most popular variety of tea in countries like the U.S. and England, green tea and oolong tea are most popular in China. What the average American thinks of as tea is thus very different from the kind of teas most Chinese drink, which have a completely different taste from black tea's. The American habit of drinking tea made from tea bags is anathema to the Chinese, who consider tea in that form to be akin to eating canned fruit rather than fresh. The word for "tea" in every language traces back to the Chinese word owing to tea's origin in China. However, the exact word used varies depending on the route by which tea reached each country or region. For example, the word in Western European languages, including English, derives from the word *tê* ("tee") in the Amoy dialect, since Western European traders brought Chinese tea to the West from the port of Xiamen in Fujian Province where the Amoy dialect was spoken. However, the Portuguese traders in the 16th century brought tea from the ports of Macau and Hong Kong to India, and they learned the word for the beverage in the Cantonese dialect, which is *cha*. This pronunciation was adopted by the Persians, who added to it their own grammatical suffix *-yi*. They then passed on the word as *chai* to become a part of many other languages including Urdu, Turkish, Russian, and Arabic.

10

● ●

Silk Production

The history of silk dates from around five thousand years ago in China, when the Chinese discovered how to boil the cocoons of the mulberry silk worm to produce fine strands of thread to make into garments. The production of silk was limited to China for the subsequent three millennia, and China maintained an almost complete monopoly of silk production until around a thousand years ago.

Silk through the ages has not just been used to make fine clothing for the upper classes--with the color of the garments indicating social rank--but was also used as a writing surface before the Chinese invented paper-making.

Originally the raising of silk worms was restricted to women, with a great many women involved in the silk-making industry. For the first thousand years, due to its lustrous appearance, only the emperor and his highest officials had the right to wear silk clothing. Over time other classes in Chinese society were allowed to wear it. It was not until the Qing dynasty (1644–1911) that the same right was extended to peasants.

One of the myriad great discoveries of ancient China was paper-making. Several centuries before Christ the Chinese were making paper out of many different materials, including silk. Paper made from silk became the first kind of luxury paper. Ancient treatises written on silk have been discovered that deal with subjects ranging from medicine to meteorology. The Chinese character for "paper," 紙, is written with the "silk" radical (糸) on the left side; the element shows a silk worm cocoon and is found in many characters related to silk. The Chinese characters for the colors "red" (紅), "green" (緑), and "purple" (紫) are also written with the "silk" radical on either the left side or bottom of the character.

During the Han dynasty (206 BC–AD 220) silk was used to pay government officials and as a reward to citizens who had distinguished themselves in some way. The length of silk cloth became a monetary standard similar to how the weight of gold was used in the West. For many centuries silk was the main diplomatic gift that the Chinese emperor would offer to the heads of neighboring kingdoms. Just as Roman soldiers were paid part of their salary in salt, Chinese soldiers were paid in bundles of plain silk, which circulated as currency in Han times. To this day, the word for "salary" in Japanese, 給料, is written with the "silk" radical on the left side of the first character in the compound.

The Chinese began exporting silk to other countries as early as three thousand years ago. Silk was discovered in the tomb of a mummy in Egypt that dates from 1070 BC. The ancient Greeks and Romans referred to the people of the distant kingdom of China as "Seres," meaning "people of silk."

A trading route leading from China to the lands far to the west was opened by the Chinese in the 2nd century AD. The main road started in the capital city of Chang-an, which is the city of Xian today, and led west by going either north or south of the Taklamakan Desert, one of the world's most arid regions, before crossing the Pamir Mountains. This route that allowed caravans of Chinese merchants to exchange silk for commodities in lands as far away as Rome came to be known as the Silk Road.

These caravans needed to travel for a year from Xian to reach the coastal areas of the Mediterranean, so they were therefore usually quite large, with anywhere from a hundred to five hundred people along with camels and yaks. A southern route led to Yemen, Burma, and India before connecting with the northern route that led to the west.

Not long after Rome conquered Egypt in 30 BC there came to be a regular flow of commerce between the Romans and Asia. The Romans developed a fondness for silk cloth coming from China. The Roman Senate unsuccessfully tried to prohibit the wearing of silk, because the import of Chinese silk meant that great amounts of gold were being drained from Rome in exchange.

Despite the demand for silk in Europe and in most of Asia, China for many centuries was able to maintain a virtual monopoly on silk production. Its secrets were protected by an imperial decree, condemning to death anyone who tried to export silkworms or their eggs. It was only around AD 300 that a Japanese expedition managed to smuggle out some silkworm eggs along with four young Chinese girls, whom they forced to teach them the process of creating silk. Diplomatic exchanges between China in the 8th and 9th centuries also allowed the Japanese to learn various techniques of silk production.

The Arabs, through their expanding conquests beginning in the 8th century AD, spread knowledge of silk production across the shores of the Mediterranean, where it took root in Spain, Italy, and North Africa. The Crusades helped introduce silk production to Western Europe, particularly to various Italian cities, which resulted in an economic boom exporting silk from there to the rest of Europe. Manufacturing was improved in the Middle Ages using the spinning wheel, and in the 16th century the French were also able to develop a successful silk trade.

The Industrial Revolution beginning in the 18th century allowed for innovations in spinning cotton, which made cotton far less expensive to produce and led to less demand for silk. However, new techniques for weaving silk gradually made silk production more efficient as well, although the silk industry in Europe was not able to compete with that for cotton. By the 20th century China and Japan regained their earlier dominance in silk production, and China has now once again become the world's largest producer of silk, accounting for close to three-quarters of worldwide production. Nevertheless, with the introduction of new fabrics like nylon, silk is once again seen as a rare luxury good and is far less important than during its golden age a great many centuries ago.

One of the very few words in the English language that derives from the Chinese language is the word "silk," which comes from the Chinese word *si*. When English speakers say the word for this beautiful material they are unwittingly acknowledging it was China that introduced silk to the world.

11

● ●

Porcelain

It is generally believed that the Chinese invented porcelain in the first century AD. Indeed, the word often used as

a synonym for "porcelain" is "china." The earliest porcelain was made by firing various items made of clay at very high temperatures. Pieces of porcelain still preserved from those early years are so durable that they have retained the bright colors and translucent quality they originally possessed.

During the Tang dynasty (AD 618–907) tea drinking became increasingly popular. This created a demand for durable and beautiful drinking vessels, leading to increased production of porcelain. At the same time trade with the lands to the west via the Silk Road grew, which led to the export of porcelain to other countries, further spurring production.

The most famous and popular porcelains produced in China during this era were of two types. "Xing" porcelain, produced in Hebei Province in the north, was very hard and white and became the standard for all Tang porcelain. The other favorite was "celadon," which varied in color from a jade green to a blue-green; it was produced in the southeastern part of China that is now Zhejiang Province.

In 1004, early in the Song dynasty (960–1279), the emperor Zhenzong appointed Jingdezhen in Jiangxi Province as the center for the production of porcelain for the court. It remained the principal imperial production center for nine hundred years. Jingdezhen became famous for its blue-colored porcelain, created by adding cobalt to kaolin clay from the deposits so abundant in that area of China.

In the first decade of the 17th century the Dutch seized Portuguese ships carrying thousands of pieces of Chinese porcelain to Europe. When this shipment was auctioned off, it sparked a craze for Chinese porcelain across Europe. Porcelain items sold for such high prices that pieces of white porcelain came to be called "white gold."

In the late 17th century, the Qing emperor Kangxi ordered his officials to carefully supervise the imperial porcelain factory in Jingdezhen. Orders were now coming in from overseas. The upper classes and even royalty in Europe and America placed special custom orders to Jingdezhen, requesting a great variety of designs that they wished to have reproduced as porcelain items.

It wasn't until the 18th century that Europeans discovered for themselves how to produce porcelain. But Chinese porcelain continued to be valued very highly in both Europe and in the Arab world. The porcelain art of China was seen as exotic, the colors were particularly bright and beautifully translucent, the works were durable and functional, and the pieces remained relatively inexpensive to buy.

Classic Chinese Texts

THE CONFUCIAN CLASSICS (NINE IN ALL)

"The Five Classics" (basis of the imperial examinations for nearly two millennia)
Yi Jing (known in English as the *I Ching* or "Book of Changes"), a divination manual; 9th century B.C.

Shi Jing ("Poetry Classic"), a book of 305 poems dating from the 11th to 7th centuries B.C.

Li Ji ("Record of Rites"), definitions of ritual terms as well as details of the life and teachings of Confucius, compiled sometime before the 3rd century B.C.

Shu Jing ("Classic of History"), different historical records from various periods but compiled sometime in the 4th or 5th century B.C.

Chunqiu ("The Spring and Autumn Annals"), the official chronicle of the Kingdom of Lu, covering a 241-year period from 722 to 481 B.C.

"The Four Books" (the classic Confucian texts also used as the basis for the imperial examinations)
Lunyu ("The Analects" of Confucius), a book of sayings attributed to Confucius as recorded by his disciples from the 5th to 3rd centuries B.C.

Mengzi ("Mencius"), a collection of political dialogues attributed to the most famous Confucian philosopher after Confucius himself; ca. 300 B.C.

Zhongyong ("The Doctrine of the Mean"), a book that teaches the path to Confucian virtue; ca. 5th century B.C.

Daxue ("The Great Learning"), a book about education and self-cultivation; ca. 5th century B.C.

DAOIST (TAOIST) CLASSIC BOOKS

Dao De Jing (better known in English as the *Tao Te Ching*), attributed to Lao Zi, a philosophical guide that advocated a laissez-faire approach for rulers as well as promoting a life in harmony with nature; 6th century B.C.

Zhuang Zi (better known in English as the *Chuang Tzu*), a large collection of anecdotes and parables, often humorous or irreverent in nature, that emphasize freedom from the human world and its conventions; 3rd century B.C.

THE FOUR GREAT NOVELS

Romance of the Three Kingdoms, a romantic dramatization of the battle for power between powerful feudal lords after the fall of the Han Dynasty; attributed to Luo Guanzhong, 14th century A.D.

Journey to the West, a fictional account of the legendary pilgrimage of the Tang Dynasty Buddhist monk Xuanzang, who traveled to India to obtain sacred Buddhist texts, aided in the novel by a monkey with magical powers; Wu Cheng'en, 16th century A.D.

Water Margin, adventures of a band of 108 outlaws who heroically battle corrupt officials during the Song Dynasty;

Shi Nai'an, 16th century A.D.

Dream of the Red Chamber, the story of the rise and fall of a powerful aristocratic family during the Qin Dynasty; Tsao Xueqin, 1791 A.D.

12

●●●●●●●●●●●●●●●●●●●●●●●●●●●●●●

Great Chinese Inventions

From many centuries before Christ until the 19th century AD China was the richest and most technologically advanced nation in the world. When it failed to develop the kind of Industrial Revolution that European countries did in the 1800s, it fell behind the West and came to be viewed as backward and weak. However, during the two thousand years that China was the world's greatest continuing high civilization, the Chinese produced thousands upon thousands of inventions that have improved our lives.

You often hear about China's four great inventions—paper-making, printing, gunpowder, and the compass. But ancient China contributed countless other things to the world. Here are but a few of them, many of which you probably didn't realize originally came from China.

1. Paper-making

By 105 AD the Chinese had already developed paper-making. The Han dynasty court official Cai Lun (AD 50–121) is credited with making the first paper. He experimented using the bark of trees, pieces of hemp cloth, plant fibers, and even fishing nets. During the 8th century Chinese paper-making spread to the Arab world, where mills were set up to make money as well as paper. Finally in the 19th century Europeans invented paper-making from wood.

2. Movable-type Printing

In European countries and in America we learn that it was the German Johannes Gutenberg who invented the printing press in 1439. The Chinese had already invented movable-type printing several centuries earlier than that. Woodblock printing was a widely used technique as early as the Tang dynasty (AD 618–907), but it was expensive and time-consuming. In the Song dynasty (960–1279) a man named Bi Sheng (990–1051) invented movable-type printing, which was quicker and easier. He carved individual characters on pieces of clay and then hardened them with fire. His invention spread rapidly across Europe and beyond.

3. Gunpowder

The Chinese invented gunpowder by accident around the year AD 1000. Taoist alchemists had been trying to create a potion to make people immortal by mixing the elements of sulfur, charcoal, and saltpeter, which unexpectedly caused a tiny explosion. It is generally believed that gunpowder helped the Mongols conquer China along with much of Asia and Europe in the 1200s. The Chinese used the invention of gunpowder mainly for firecrackers while Europeans created cannons and guns, which they then used to conquer people in lands across the globe.

4. Compasses

The Chinese invented the compass sometime between the 2nd century BC and the 1st century AD. Since a compass indicates directions, the Chinese first used it in orienting the layout of buildings. By AD 1000 compasses were commonly used on Chinese ships, enabling them to navigate. Arab traders sailing to China learned of the compass and brought it to the West.

5. Mechanical Clocks

The world's first mechanical clock was invented in AD 725 by Yi Xing, a Chinese Buddhist monk. It was operated by dripping water that powered a wheel making one revolution every 24 hours. Hundreds of years later, in 1092, the inventor Su Song developed a more sophisticated clock 200 years before the first mechanical clock was created in Europe.

6. Umbrellas

The ancient Egyptians did invent a parasol (a type of umbrella to protect against the sun) as early as 3,500 years ago. However, because Egypt has such a dry climate, the Egyptians never found a need to waterproof their parasols and create umbrellas. It was the Chinese in the 11th century BC who created the first true waterproof umbrellas, for which they used silk. At first umbrellas were only used by the nobles and the royal family.

7. Acupuncture

The oldest Chinese medicine book, written 2,300 years ago, talks about acupuncture, which indicates that this therapy was widely used in China long before that book was written. Acupuncture involves the skillful placing of needles in the pressure points of the human body to relieve pain. Various kinds of acupuncture needles were discovered in the tomb of Prince Liu Sheng, who died around 200 BC. This is further proof that acupuncture was already in use in China more than two thousand years ago

8. Earthquake Detectors

According to court records of the Han dynasty a seismograph for learning the direction and force of an earthquake was created in AD 132 by the brilliant inventor Zhang Heng (78–140). In AD 138 the Chinese using this instrument learned that an earthquake was happening in a city around 600 miles away. This was the first time that people were able to detect an earthquake. Modern seismographs only began to be created in 1848 in Europe.

9. Rockets

Ancient Chinese inventors created rockets powered by ignited gunpowder. In AD 228 the Chinese kingdom of Wei was already using torches attached to arrows to protect one of their cities against the invading troops of another kingdom. Later the Song dynasty (960–1279) adapted gunpowder to make rockets. A paper tube stuffed with gunpowder was attached to an arrow that could be launched by a bow. This kind of ancient rocket was widely used in China by the military but also for entertainment.

10. Kites

The Chinese developed the kite around three thousand years ago. The earliest kites were made of wood. In early times kites were mainly used for military purposes such as sending messages, measuring distances, testing the wind, and signaling. Over time kite flying became a fun pastime that is now enjoyed by people all over the world.

11. Toothbrushes

The Chinese invented the bristle toothbrush in 1498. They made toothbrushes with coarse horse hair attached to bone or bamboo handles. The invention was later brought to the New World by Europeans.

12. Paper Money

More than a thousand years ago the Chinese became the first to develop paper money. By the end of the 8th or beginning of the 9th century AD they were already using folding paper money. Paper bills were originally used as privately issued bills of credit or exchange notes. A merchant would deposit his cash in the capital and then receive an official piece of paper that he could exchange for metal coins in other cities.

13. Wheelbarrows

The single-wheeled cart we call the wheelbarrow was invented by Prime Minister Zhuge Liang in AD 231, according to a famous Chinese history book. He called his device a "wooden ox." It was designed to carry men and weapons into battle. However, there are paintings of men using wheelbarrows in tombs in southwestern China that date as far back as AD 118. The wheelbarrow didn't arrive in Europe until sometime between the late 1100s and the early 1200s.

***

Chinese are responsible for countless inventions that have helped shape the history of the world, of which the above are but a few. Ironically, because China never rewarded inventors the way they were rewarded in Europe, it was the European governments who promoted and developed these inventions and then used them to colonize much of the world, including parts of China.

13

● ●

Martial Arts

The origin of the martial arts in China most likely goes back as far as four thousand years ago. They were created as a means of self-defense as well as part of military training. Hand-to-hand combat and practice with weapons have been taught to Chinese soldiers for thousands of years.

Several hundred fighting styles have been developed over the centuries, but the general terms for martial arts in China are "kung fu" (pronounced "guhng-fu" and spelled *gōngfu* in pinyin; written as 功夫) and "wushu" (*wǔshù* in pinyin; written as 武术).

The first standardized form of kungfu is said to have come from the Shaolin Temple in the mountains of Henan Province, built in AD 495. Several of the earliest Buddhist monks who lived there were highly skilled in martial arts and created their own formalized style. There is evidence that Shaolin monks used this fighting style to help defend the monastery from bandits around AD 610. The Shaolin monks continue to practice their particular brand of martial arts to this day. Students come from all over China and from many foreign countries to learn Shaolin kungfu from the masters there, in addition to the one million tourists who visit the temple annually.

Most fighting styles practiced as traditional Chinese martial arts today reached their popularity during the 20th century. These include Bagua, Praying Mantis, Fujian White Crane, and Taijiquan (incorrectly called "Tai chi" in English).

These styles have become popular with the general public over the course of the last hundred years.

In 1900 anger at the foreigners who occupied areas of the major cities in China caused an uprising against the foreigners by a large group of peasants calling themselves "the Righteous and Harmonious Fists." Such was the Chinese belief in the power of kungfu that the rebels believed that the brand of kungfu they practiced would protect them from the bullets fired from the guns of the foreigners. This uprising is known in the West as the Boxer Rebellion due to the martial arts practiced by the rebels. Although kungfu did not make the rebels invincible and the rebellion failed miserably, the episode does indicate how widely Chinese martial arts were practiced at the time.

During the Japanese invasion and the Chinese civil war in the 1930s and 1940s, Chinese martial arts spread to the general public, as many martial artists were encouraged to openly teach their art. Some also considered martial arts as a means to promote national pride and build a strong nation. Many training manuals were published, a training academy was created, two national examinations were organized to test martial arts ability, and demonstration teams traveled overseas to give performances.

In the late 1970s and through the 1980s, the most popular spectator sport in China was wushu. Huge audiences would fill stadiums to watch professional martial arts spar with one another in a gymnastic display of mock hand-to-hand combat, often with weapons like blunt spears and dull swords.

In modern times, Chinese martial arts have inspired a whole host of kungfu films. The films of Bruce Lee in the 1970s helped create great interest in the martial arts in America. Around the same time a TV Western series called *Kung Fu* also served to popularize Chinese martial arts in the U.S. With sixty episodes over a three-year period, it was the first

American TV show that tried to convey the philosophy and practice of the Chinese martial arts.

Martial artists and actors such as Jet Li and Jackie Chan have continued to make kungfu popular around the world through their films, with Jackie Chan even adding a sense of humor to the fight scenes in his movies. Chinese and Taiwanese martial arts films like *Crouching Tiger, Hidden Dragon* (2000), *Hero* (2002), *House of Flying Daggers* (2004), and *Reign of Assassins* (2010) have met with great success internationally.

A great many Chinese practice martial arts in China today. Since China is a far safer society than the U.S. and crime rates are relatively very low, the Chinese generally don't study martial arts to protect themselves as so many Americans do. They do it instead for relaxation and to relieve stress. The gentle forms of qigong and taijiquan are especially popular with older people as a way to maintain balance and muscle strength. Large groups of elderly people in China are often seen in the public parks in the mornings practicing qigong and taijiquan together, led by an instructor. Some groups or individuals will do these slow, meditative exercises barehanded, while others will do them holding dull swords or large fans.

Qigong (pronounced "chee-guhng"; *qìgōng* in pinyin; written as 气功) literally means "Life Energy Cultivation" and is a practice of slow flowing movements, deep rhythmic breathing, and a calm meditative state of mind. A great many Chinese believe that it promotes health by cultivating and balancing your *qi*, or "life energy."

Taijiquan (pronounced "ty-jee-chwe-en"; *tàijíquán* in pinyin; written as 太极拳) is an internal Chinese martial art practiced for both its defense training and its health benefits. It is incorrectly called Tai Chi in the West. The term *taiji* literally means "Great Ultimate." The goal is that by practicing taijiquan you will come to feel a unity with the ultimate creative force of the universe that we in the West perhaps think of as "God." Originally created as a martial art, it is more commonly practiced by ordinary Chinese today for health reasons. When done as a gentle exercise, taijiquan is performed with rather slow movements to bring about a sense of calm and well-being. Taijiquan also helps older people maintain their balance late in life.

Japanese martial arts such as karate, judo, aikido, and jujutsu, and Korean martial arts such as taekwondo, were all originally inspired by the Chinese martial arts.

14

The Real Origins of Bonsai, Tofu, and Koi

So many of the things we in the West believe originated in Japan were actually borrowed by the Japanese from China many centuries ago. English speakers know them by their Japanese names largely because the U.S. occupied Japan from 1945 to 1952. What in English as well as Japanese are called "bonsai," "tofu," and "koi" were all cultural borrowings from the much older civilization of China.

To be fair, these well-known aspects of Asian culture all came to Japan over a thousand years ago, and the Japanese have adapted them and made them their own. But few people in the West are aware of the enormous debt that Japanese culture owes to China, a debt the Japanese themselves are hesitant to acknowledge.

Particularly during the Nara period of Japanese history, from AD 710 to 794, the Japanese modeled their culture after that of the Chinese, who were much more advanced in almost every way. The Japanese adopted Chinese characters to produce their writing system, embraced Buddhism as the principal religion, and began to imitate Chinese dress. It was around this time that Japan learned rice cultivation from the Chinese, as well as the use of chopsticks. The Japanese capital city of Nara, from which the name for this historical period is derived, was built on the model of Chang-an, the capital city of China at the time.

Bonsai, tofu, and koi ponds are actually among the lesser

cultural items the Japanese learned from the Chinese. Bonsai is the art of growing miniature trees or shrubs in small containers or pots. The dwarf trees and flowering shrubs are grown from regular stock. Through pruning, root reduction, grafting, and other techniques, the resulting trees imitate the shape and form of full-size, mature trees, but in miniature. The word "bonsai" is written with the Chinese characters 盆 ("bon"), meaning a pot, and 栽 ("sai"), meaning planting. Those same characters are pronounced *pénzāi* in the original Chinese, from which the term originates. It can be argued that the Japanese adaptation of this Chinese horticultural art has surpassed that of China in its variety and subtlety. Nevertheless, the Japanese and the world should acknowledge the ingenuity of the ancient Chinese in creating this exquisite art form in the first place.

What is known as tofu in Japan as well as in English-speaking countries also originated in China, where it is called *dòufu*. The word literally means "beans" (*dòu*) that are "corrupted/

curdled" (*fǔ*) and is written in both Chinese and Japanese as 豆腐. This food, which only became well known in the West in the past few decades, is made from coagulating soy milk and then pressing the curds that result into soft, white blocks. *Dòufu* (tofu) is a great source of vegetable protein that health-conscious people in the West know to be a healthier alternative to animal protein. There are many different kinds of tofu. The Japanese prefer a variety that is extremely soft and gelatinous ("silken tofu"), which they often put in soups. The Chinese use a wide variety of different textures of tofu, including a firmer variety that can hold up better when stir-fried, which they put into various dishes that include seafood or vegetables.

According to Chinese legend, this soy-based food product was invented by Prince Liu An, who lived in the second century BC. *Dòufu* (tofu) and the technique of producing it were introduced to both Japan and Korea during the Nara period, around the same time as the cultivation of bonsai. It is perhaps no coincidence that the introduction of tofu into Japan and Korea coincided with the spread of Buddhism to those countries, since Buddhism in East Asia traditionally advocates a vegetarian diet. An alternative to animal protein was, therefore, essential. Tofu is high not only in protein content, but also in iron and calcium.

Koi is the Japanese term for decorative varieties of domestically raised carp. They are often seen in the outdoor ponds of Japanese gardens in the West as well as in gardens all over Japan, most famously on the grounds of many Japanese Buddhist temples and Shinto shrines. The word "koi" is written with the Chinese character 鯉 for "carp." Like bonsai and tofu, the cultivation of koi and the creation of ponds to show them off originated in China more than a thousand years ago.

The "common carp" was raised for food as early as the fifth century AD in China. In Hangzhou in southeast China these carp were bred for color mutations over a thousand years ago. The selective breeding of this fish led to the gradual creation of the goldfish. Because carp are able to survive in many different climates with a wide range of water conditions, it was possible for the Japanese to import the domesticated carp from China.

Carp were first bred for color in Japan during the early part of the 19th century, initially on the northwest coast of the main island of Honshu. By the 20th century, the Japanese started to breed new color patterns, including red, yellow, blue, white, cream, and black. The most famous color pattern they created, however, was that of the red and white carp known as *kōhaku* (literally, "red-white").

The rest of the world outside of Japan did not become aware of the various color variations the Japanese had bred into koi until 1914. That was the year many varieties of koi raised in northwestern Honshu were shown at the Tokyo Exposition. This ignited great interest across the country and gradually led to the cultivation of these beautiful fish becoming popular worldwide.

While it must be acknowledged that the Japanese have made significant adaptations to Chinese cultural items such as koi and bonsai, it's also only fair to recognize that these wonderful gifts to the world originated in China, a civilization far older than Japan.

15

The U.S. Opium Trade with China

From the late 17th century through the early 19th century, Great Britain suffered a huge trade imbalance with China. The British had come to rely on huge imports of tea from China, while there was little the Chinese wanted to import from Great Britain. The result was a serious depletion of British silver reserves that threatened the health of the British economy. The solution the British hit upon was to obtain a huge quantity of opium from the one million opium farmers in their colony of India and export it to China, with the goal of making the Chinese as addicted to the drug as the British had become dependent on Chinese tea.

The Chinese emperor had declared opium to be illegal in his country. To avoid criticism in Britain should the British sell opium directly to China, the government instead sold opium in Calcutta to a private enterprise, the East India Company. With the protection of the British navy, East India Company ships would haul the contraband drug to the southeastern Chinese coast, where Chinese criminals, in cahoots with corrupt local Chinese officials, would row out to receive the English opium and bring it to shore.

When the Chinese government attempted to prevent this horribly addictive and destructive drug from flooding its shores, the British instigated not one but two wars, from 1839 to 1842 and from 1856 to 1860. By winning both conflicts the British ensured they could continue the opium trade with

impunity. They also forced the Chinese government to pay a huge indemnity and to cede to them the harbor city of Hong Kong, in addition to granting them five treaty ports from where they could continue to operate.

When American merchants in the early 19th century saw the tremendous profits that the British were enjoying from the opium trade, they wanted to participate in the spoils. Few Americans realize how much of the wealth of their country in the 19th century derived from the huge amount of money many prominent Americans made by selling opium to China. Opium merchants like John Murray Forbes, Samuel Russell, Thomas Perkins, John Perkins Cushing, William Henry Low, and Warren Delano (grandfather of Franklin Delano Roosevelt) all made their fortunes through the opium trade in China.

The Perkins family used part of their money to build Massachusetts General Hospital. Much of the land on which Yale University was built was provided by the Russell family from profits made by helping hook the Chinese on that harmful drug called opium. And Franklin Delano Roosevelt was able to enjoy a fairly luxurious life not on the money he made from holding public office but from the money he inherited from his grandfather, Warren Delano.

Warren Delano made a large fortune trading opium in Canton Province in southeastern China. Delano first went to China at age twenty-four to work for Russell & Company, which had pioneered trading with China. There he joined up with John Perkins Cushing, also a partner in Russell & Company, who had established a working relationship with a Chinese official named Howqua. Together they set up an anchored floating warehouse off the coast of Canton, so that their ships could unload their opium before continuing up the Pearl River Delta to deliver their contraband.

In recognition of the great harm opium had caused in their country, the Communist Chinese government outlawed its growth and consumption in the 1950s, during their first decade of rule. As many as ten million addicts were forced to undergo treatment. Producers and dealers were executed, and areas that had been growing opium were planted with new crops.

16

The First Educational Mission

In recent years much attention has been given in the U.S. media to the rapidly increasing number of students from China entering American high schools, colleges, and universities. Few Americans are aware that the first influx of Chinese students occurred as early as 1872, albeit in far smaller numbers than today.

A young Chinese man from Guangdong (Canton) Province named Yung Wing was one of the very first people from China to receive an education in a Western country. As a boy Yung Wing had studied at the Morrison mission school near Canton; he then continued his education at Monson Academy in Massachusetts and eventually entered Yale University. When he returned to China in 1854, he began to lobby Chinese government officials to provide funding to send a contingent of Chinese boys to America to receive a modern Western education. His hope was that after graduation these young Chinese would acquire knowledge of superior American technology and return to their country to help it modernize.

Yung Wing's idea was ignored until it reached the ears of a Chinese official who saw the pressing need to modernize the Chinese military in the face of the threat posed by the vastly superior militaries of Western nations. Great Britain, for example, had already dealt China devastating defeats in the two Opium Wars (1839–42 and 1856–60). These conflicts had shocked Chinese officials into realizing that their weaponry was too antiquated and their transportation systems inadequate to meet the needs of modern warfare.

In the summer of 1872 a group of thirty Chinese boys, ranging in age from twelve to twenty, set sail for America. The goal of the Chinese Educational Mission, as it was dubbed, was to have these boys study Western science and engineering in New England. After fifteen years in America, they were to return home for careers in service to the Chinese government, designing and building telegraph systems, railroads, and warships and other armaments.

Yung Wing and an older, much more conservative Chinese official accompanied the boys as supervisors. Another 30 boys were sent in each of the following three years, so that by 1875 there was a total of 120 Chinese boys receiving their education in America. The majority of these students came from Yung Wing's native province of Guangdong, with smaller contingents from Fujian Province, Shanghai, and other coastal cities.

These boys were housed with American families in Hartford, Connecticut, where they enrolled in local public high schools to prepare them for American universities. In the late 1870s as many as forty-three Chinese youths entered American colleges. Of these, twenty enrolled in Yale University and eight at M.I.T. While some chose to study science or engineering, others elected to pursue the humanities or social sciences.

Unfortunately this Chinese experiment of sending young people to study in the U.S. ended abruptly in 1881, nine years before the end date originally planned. There were several reasons for the sudden termination. For one, the very conservative Chinese official who with Yung Wing was overseeing the mission had been warning his government that the boys were becoming too Americanized and were losing their Chinese identity.

The most important factor in bringing an end to the mission was the rising anti-Chinese sentiment in the U.S. There was growing resentment among American workers toward the Chinese immigrants they perceived as a threat to their jobs. Although Chinese workers made up only 0.00005% of the entire American workforce, the anti-Chinese feelings of American labor led to passage of the Chinese Exclusion Act of 1882, which banned any further immigration from China.

The official end of the Chinese Educational Mission came after a small group of Chinese students who had applied to enter West Point and the Naval Academy in Annapolis were flatly refused. This, despite the students being eminently qualified, violated the Burlingame-Seward Treaty that the U.S. government had previously signed with China. One of the treaty's provisions said that the citizens of each country should have reciprocal access to education and schooling within each other's borders. The Chinese government was deeply offended by what was an obvious violation of the treaty. It withdrew its support for the mission and ordered Yung Wing and the students to return immediately to China.

Although this first experiment in international education had been cut short, the mission still produced some notable successes. After their return to China, many of the students made significant contributions to their homeland. The MIT-trained students alone were instrumental in developing a railway system in China and in modernizing the mining industry; they contributed to the development of a telegraph system in China and became leaders in agricultural reform, business, and other endeavors. Other students in the program rose to positions of great prominence in the Chinese government, although their efforts at reform failed in the face of a ruling class averse to change.

In their wonderful book *Fortunate Sons: The 120 Chinese Boys Who Came To America, Went to School, and Revolutionized an Ancient Civilization,* Liel Leibovitz and Matthew Miller emphasize that Yung Wing and the 120 students who made up the mission represented a significantly more privileged community than the great majority of their fellow Chinese immigrants. Those countrymen instead came to work in low-wage and dangerous jobs, on the railroads out west or in New York. Almost all lived in crowded Chinatown tenements. They were forced to endure bigotry and scorn in their communities and in the media.

In striking contrast, Yung and the mission students studied at some of New England's leading institutions, living with well-to-do host families and in Ivy League dormitories. They enjoyed the support of both the US and Chinese governments. Yet, when relations between the two countries turned sour, Yung Wing and the students were just as vulnerable and threatened as any of their fellow immigrants.

17

● ●

Chinese Immigration to the U.S.

There has been the common belief in the U.S. that America has always welcomed immigrants from all over the world, including China.

This, sadly, is simply not true. When America was founded, the concept of "illegal immigration" did not exist. However, in 1882 Congress passed the Chinese Exclusion Act, which prohibited any Chinese from entering the U.S. It was the only time in American history that people were forbidden from entering the country based *solely* on their nationality or racial identity until 2017, when the Trump administration issued a ban on travel for citizens of certain Muslim countries. Under the act, Chinese already living in the U.S. were excluded from citizenship and from owning property and became permanent aliens.

This exclusionary law was passed in response to a growing perception on the part of white workers in America in the 1860s and '70s that the Chinese were unfair competition and were stealing their jobs. Before the California Gold Rush in 1849 there were only around fifty Chinese living in all of the U.S. By 1852, with the promise of gold, and that of a free country where anyone willing to work hard could do well, as many as twenty thousand Chinese had migrated to America.

The Chinese immigrants mined more efficiently and saved more of their earnings than did the white miners. In the 1860s when European immigrants proved unable to dig through the hard granite rock of the Sierra Nevadas to lay track for the Transcontinental Railroad, the Chinese workers took over the task and succeeded. That task included the most dangerous job of digging into the cliffs and placing charges of dynamite to create passageways in the mountains, and it cost as many as 150 Chinese their lives. And yet when the opening of the railroad was celebrated in May 1869, no Chinese were invited to be present alongside their white coworkers.

When the railroad was completed, the Chinese workers spread out across the West, where they opened hotels and restaurants and laundries, as well as taking up farming. Because they were generally much more frugal and hard-working, they often produced higher-quality goods and services than did their Caucasian competitors.

This was particularly angering, since the whites perceived the Chinese as a much lesser race. Competition from the inferior "Orientals" had to be eliminated, either by law or, if necessary, by force. Unions, including the Knights of Labor, demanded that "the Chinese must go!"

The Chinese Exclusion Act empowered vigilante groups in the American West to strike out against the Chinese already living in their communities. In September 1885, in the coal-mining town of Rock Springs, Wyoming, several hundred white men surrounded the Chinatown where many hundreds of Chinese lived and began shooting indiscriminately, killing men, women, and children. Those Chinese whom they didn't kill fled for their lives. All the homes and shops that had belonged to the Chinese were burned to the ground. None of the sixteen white miners later charged with arson and murder were ever convicted. Earlier that same year, the Seattle police chief backed by an armed mob forced all the Chinese in Seattle's Chinatown to a wharf, where they were sent off to sea at gunpoint. Similar incidents occurred in Utah, New Mexico, and Alaska.

Ironically in 1886, only four years after the Chinese Exclusion Act was passed, the Statue of Liberty was dedicated in New York harbor. On its pedestal were the words "Give me your tired, your poor, your huddled masses yearning to breathe free, the wretched refuse of your teeming shore." The Exclusion Act was originally intended to be in effect only for ten years. It was renewed, however, in 1892 and 1902 and remained in effect until 1943. And in the two decades following 1943, only 105 Chinese were allowed to emigrate to the U.S. each year. For over eighty years few Americans would ever come in contact with a Chinese person.

18

Chiang Kai-shek

Chiang Kai-shek, the Chinese leader whom the U.S. supported from the 1920s through the 1970s as the representative of "democratic China," was actually a ruthless authoritarian dictator and a crook. Chiang, as the head of the Kuomintang (Nationalist) Party of China, in the early 1920s led his forces together with those of Mao Zedong's Communist followers in a military campaign to wrest control of central China from local warlords. After successfully collaborating with the Communists, in April 1927 Chiang carried out one of the bloodiest betrayals in history by massacring between twenty and thirty thousand presumed Communists in Shanghai, with hundreds of thousands more slaughtered in the countryside.

When Japan invaded the three northeasternmost provinces of China known as Manchuria, rather than attempt to drive back the invading Japanese army Chiang chose instead to pursue a campaign against the Communists, who had fled to China's northwest. Chiang believed that Japan's army was too strong to be defeated, and he feared losses to his own Nationalist troops, which he wanted to save for his fight against Mao.

In ruling central China in the 1920s and 30s Chiang did nothing to alleviate the sad plight of the Chinese peasants, who made up well over 90% of the population. Rather than reducing the terrible burden on the peasants—most of whom had been reduced to working as tenant farmers for rich landlords who taxed them severely—Chiang showed favor only to the wealthy urban class. Mirroring Fascist leaders in other countries, in early 1932 Chiang had six young writers who had criticized him arrested and buried alive; this was but one of thousands of executions and assassinations of writers and intellectuals Chiang ordered against those he felt threatened his regime.

In early December 1930, Chiang led his Nationalist troops in an attack on the area of China held by Mao and his followers. Generalissimo Chiang largely appointed the sons of landlords to be his officers. His soldiers were so poorly paid and so badly supplied that they survived by plundering the homes of the peasants. This caused them to be so despised by the great majority of Chinese people that Chiang had to resort to kidnaping in order to man his army. These shanghaied men were tied together with ropes around their necks and marched hundreds of miles from their villages and stripped naked at night to prevent them running away.

Ignorant of Chiang Kai-shek's brutal methods, the U.S. government viewed the Generalissimo as a Chinese hero who would lead China to become a free and democratic nation modeled after the United States, and our great ally in Asia. Henry Luce, the magazine mogul who launched the magazines *Time, Life,* and *Fortune,* helped create an image of Chiang in American minds as a noble, dashing, and brave figure—a Chinese George Washington, beloved by the Chinese people. Luce even declared Chiang *Time* magazine's "Man of the Year" in 1937. This was the same year that Japan occupied Shanghai and most of eastern China, while Chiang chose to retreat with his huge army to the mountainous area of Sichuan Province in the remote southwest rather than attempt to turn back the invaders, electing to concentrate on fighting Mao.

The gross misperception of Chiang in the U.S. was due to the great ignorance about China itself both by officials at the highest level of government as well as by the American population as a whole. It was also due to a highly successful propaganda campaign orchestrated by the family into which the Generalissimo had married.

In 1927 the forty-year-old Chiang was joined in marriage to the thirty-year-old Meiling Soong in a Christian ceremony in Shanghai. Meiling had been sent to the U.S. as a young teenager to be educated and later graduated from Wellesley College. She and other members of her family had converted to Christianity in the southern Methodist tradition, and Meiling soon convinced her husband to do the same. Suddenly China's rule was in the hands of a Christian family. Meiling's ability to speak English fluently and her charming personality won over many prominent Americans in the government and the media.

Equally important in helping to create a false image of

Chiang Kai-shek as the noble leader of a "free and demo-cratic" China was the propaganda machine led by Meiling's brother, T.V. Soong. The Soong family from which Chiang's wife came was one of the wealthiest in China. Chiang's broth-er-in-law, T.V., was a Harvard graduate who served both as finance minister for the General as well as his mouthpiece with U.S. government officials. Knowing very little about the actual situation in China and ignoring the advice of the few Americans living there who warned that it was really Mao Zedong who had the allegiance of most of the Chinese people, the closest advisers to U.S. President Franklin Delano Roos-evelt were convinced that U.S. interests lay in backing Chiang Kai-shek.

After the end of World War II, civil war raged between Chiang's Nationalists and Mao's Communists. The U.S. spent an enormous amount of money providing Chiang with weap-ons and supplies out of fear of a Communist victory. Despite his far superior American weaponry Chiang was defeated by the Communist forces, who had the support of the great majority of the Chinese people. In 1949 Chiang and his follow-ers permanently withdrew to the island of Taiwan.

For a detailed and illuminating account of the American government's consistent inability to understand China over the past century and the disastrous consequences of that ignorance, consider reading the book *The China Mirage: The Hidden History of American Disaster in Asia* by James Bradley.

19

● ●

The Legacy of Mao Zedong

Not many years after Mao's death in 1976, if you asked the ordinary Chinese citizen what they thought of the Chairman, they would invariably answer "70% good, 30% bad." The uniformity of their answer betrayed the fact that they were all quoting the official Party line in evaluating the legacy of the man who had successfully led the Communist Party to power in 1949. In the West, however, Mao is generally described along with Hitler and Stalin as one of the three most villainous national rulers in the 20th century.

Unlike Hitler and Stalin, whose villainy is quite clear, Mao remains a controversial figure. He undeniably was one of the most important, influential individuals in modern world history. There are historians in both China and the West who give him credit for some major achievements. His ability to inspire and mobilize millions of his people, coupled with his brilliant military strategy, allowed his army to defeat the much better equipped Kuomintang under General Chiang Kai-shek and unify the country after three decades of ruinous civil war.

Mao restored Chinese national pride by driving out the foreign imperial powers that had been occupying various parts of China since the mid-1800s. He is praised for elevating the status of women by declaring they should have equal rights with men. Mao also provided universal education, which significantly boosted literacy. When he took power in 1949, only 20% of the population could read, compared to over 65% by the time of his death in 1976.

Mao greatly improved health care for his people. During his thirty years as leader, average life expectancy in China nearly doubled, from thirty-five to sixty-three. Population nearly doubled, too, growing from approximately 550 million to more than 900 million.

Other historians, both Chinese and Western, as well as the vast majority of Americans, condemn Mao as an autocratic ruler whose disastrous economic policies during the Great Leap Forward from 1958 to 1962 caused the deaths of tens of millions of Chinese from starvation. In an attempt to industrialize China as quickly as possible to catch up to Western nations, Mao took farmers from their own fields to live in large-scale rural communes and set them to work producing cheap and ultimately useless steel in small backyard furnaces. The misdirected energies of a large percentage of the agricultural work force, combined with lies about grain production and mismanaged distribution of food, resulted in the worst famine in human history. More than half of the people in some Chinese villages died from hunger during this time. The total number of dead between 1959 and 1961 alone is estimated to have been between thirty and forty million, equaling the current population of California.

At least as grievous was the reign of terror that Mao ordered in 1966, which he proclaimed as the "Great Cultural Revolution." After the Great Leap Forward had proved a great blunder, Mao felt threatened by his rivals in the Party leadership. Rallying to restore the revolutionary fervor that was understandably failing, he called on young men and women between the ages of fourteen and twenty-one to stamp out all traces of the old society—which he declared impediments to creating a new, modern nation—by destroying the religious and cultural artifacts of China's past.

Stirring up the youth of China to a fever pitch, he proclaimed them "Red Guards" and sent them to ferret out anyone

who might endanger the revolutionary path he had set for the country. Those he deemed enemies of the state included any "revisionist elements" among the Party leadership, rich industrialists and entrepreneurs, wealthier peasants, and most particularly intellectuals, including all teachers, i.e., anyone who wasn't either a worker or a poor peasant.

All those belonging to one of these "black elements of society," as Mao called them, were publicly humiliated as counter-revolutionaries, often beaten, and then sent to the countryside to learn from the peasants the value of hard work. Mao instituted a system of hundreds of forced labor camps throughout the country to which those deemed the most serious political dissidents were sent; these lasted from the 1950s through the 1980s, well after Mao's demise. The stated purpose of the labor camps was *lǎogǎi*, meaning "reform through labor." A great many of those forced to endure this Chinese version of the Soviet gulag died as a result of the primitive living conditions and brutal fourteen-hour work days.

All schools were closed for the first year or two of the

Cultural Revolution, which began in 1966, while universities remained closed beyond the ten years that the Cultural Revolution lasted and didn't even partially reopen until 1977, a year after Mao's death in 1976. In the late 1960s millions of students in the cities were sent to the countryside to be "re-educated" by living with and learning from the peasants. For a brief period groups of Red Guards in the cities attacked Communist Party leaders, teachers, writers, artists, musicians, and other intellectuals, as well as affluent people of property and even small shop owners or people who owned their own home. As the Cultural Revolution spiraled out of control, it wasn't long before gangs of workers formed and began to assault the entire population in a reign of terror similar to that of the French Revolution. When those marauding gangs went to war against one another and millions of people died, Mao reluctantly called in the army to stop the violence.

Despite all this, Mao Zedong continues to be viewed in China as a national hero and. At one end of Tiananmen Square in the heart of Beijing sits Mao's mausoleum, visited daily by large, respectful crowds. At the other end of the square hangs a giant portrait of Mao above the entrance to the Forbidden City, a favorite tourist site for both Chinese and foreign visitors. On December 25, 2008, China opened the Mao Zedong Square to visitors in his home town in central Hunan Province to commemorate the 115th anniversary of his birth. Mao continues to be thought of fondly by a great many people in China, mostly among the lower classes, in large part because he ensured that everyone in the society was cared for. Many taxi drivers in cities like Beijing hang small portraits of Mao from their rearview mirrors as an amulet to keep them safe while on the road.

Mao also remains the most honored figure by the Chinese Communist Party and is respected by the majority of the general population as the Founding Father of modern China who restored dignity and self-respect to the Chinese people. Though the Chinese Communist Party, which Mao led to power, has rejected in practice the economic fundamentals of much of Mao's ideology, it retains for itself many of the powers established under Mao's reign. The Party continues to control the army, the police, the law courts, and the media, and does not permit multiparty elections at the national or local level, except in Hong Kong.

In the spirit of Mao, China's Party leaders continue to oppress dissidents, from intellectuals and human rights lawyers to outspoken religious leaders and human rights activists such as Liu Xiaobo. Mao's revolutionary tactics are still emulated by insurgents in other countries, and his political ideology continues to be embraced by many Communist organizations around the world.

There is no doubt that Mao demonstrated the same repressive tendencies seen in all the authoritarian regimes of the 20th and 21st centuries. And yet it seems there will never be total agreement in either China or in the West as to the exact nature of Mao's legacy. The Chinese journalist Liu Binyan called Mao "both a monster and a genius." One former Chinese Party official declared Mao "a great historical criminal, but also a great force for good." The British historian Philip Short, in his biography of Mao published in 1999 entitled *Mao: A Life,* argues that the Chairman should not be equated with Hitler and Stalin. According to Short, the deaths caused by those dictators of Nazi Germany and Soviet Russia were largely systematic and deliberate, whereas the overwhelming majority of the deaths under Mao were unintended consequences of famine or his "reform through labor" policy. Short emphasizes that Mao did not order the deaths of those classes of people he felt were enemies of the state, due to his belief in redemption through thought reform. It should be noted that, unlike Hitler, Mao never persecuted anyone based on ethnicity or engaged in genocide. And unlike Stalin, Mao never personally ordered the execution or imprisonment of specific individuals, as Stalin did to thousands of his political enemies.

Mao's English interpreter, Sidney Rittenberg, says in his memoir entitled *The Man Who Stayed Behind* that while Mao was "a great leader in history," he was also "a great criminal" because "his wild fantasies" unintentionally led to the deaths of tens of millions of people. Philip Short summarizes Mao's rule by stating that "Mao's tragedy and his grandeur were that he remained to the end in thrall to his own revolutionary dreams.... He freed China from the straitjacket of its Confucian past, but the bright Red future he promised turned out to be a sterile purgatory."

China's Society,
Culture, and Language

20

● ●

Terms for Family Members

When something is of special importance to a culture, there is often no generic term for it. For instance, in the Chinese language there is no word for "rice." When rice is growing in the fields it's called *dàozi* (稻子). When harvested it's called *mǐ* (米). But when it's cooked, rice is called *mǐfàn* (米饭) or *báifàn* (白饭). The Japanese language has three equivalent words for rice in these various forms, with a fourth word for "rice," *raisu*, when rice is cooked in a Western-style dish like "curried rice."

In the Inuit language there is no generic word for snow. It's too important to specify whether the snow is wet or dry, fluffy or powdery, etc. And in Arabic there is no general word for "camel." There are specific words for a one-humped camel, a two-humped camel, a male camel, or a female camel. But camels are traditionally too important to Arab societies for there to be one general term for that animal. In fact, in Farsi, the language of Iran, there is a two-syllable word for a female camel that only gives milk when its nose is tickled!

Perhaps the most stunning example of such a proliferation of specific terms is the approximately 460 terms for family members in Chinese. For almost all of Chinese history up until the last few generations, the Chinese people lived in extended family groups in one family compound. Every son in the family would live his entire life with his paternal grandparents, his parents, his brothers, and his brother's children, as well as with his father's brothers and their children. The ideal was for a man to be so fortunate as to live with four generations of his family under the same roof. For girls, however, usually as soon as they reached puberty, and sometimes even before, they were married off to a family in another village or town, and might only visit their parents and brothers once a year at New Year's.

Therefore it became important for a man to specify whether his "grandfather" and "grandmother" were his father's parents, with whom he would live until they died, or his mother's parents, whom he would rarely ever see. Your paternal grandfather is your *yéye* (爷爷) and your paternal grandmother is your *năinai* (奶奶), whereas your maternal grandfather is your *wàigōng* (外公), which literally means "outside older gentleman," and your maternal grandmother is your *wàipó* (外婆), which literally means "outside older woman," since both of these grandparents live outside your family compound and, most likely, outside your village or town.

There are as many as five words each for "uncle" and for "aunt," depending on which side of the family they are on, whether they are blood relatives or related to you by marriage, and in the case of blood "uncles" on your father's side, whether they are older or younger than your father. Your uncle who is your father's older brother is your *bóbo* (伯伯), to whom both you and your parents must show special respect. Your uncle who is your father's younger brother is your *shūshu* (叔叔), whom your father has a responsibility to take care of. This reflects an important tenet of Confucian teaching, which stressed that social order should be based on a respect for seniority and which defined the obligations in the family based on age relative to others in the family. Your mother's brothers, on the other hand, whom you rarely will encounter, are your *jiùjiu* (舅舅). There are several more words for "uncle" to describe the man married to either your father's sister (*gūfū* 姑夫) or married to your mother's sister (*yífū* 姨夫).

The familial relationship with the greatest number of specific terms, however, is reserved for the relation we know in English as a "cousin." There are eight separate terms for a first cousin alone, depending on which side of the family that "cousin" is from, whether that "cousin" is male or female, and whether that "cousin" is older or younger than you. These terms stem from the fact that there is no word for "brother" or "sister" in Chinese, let alone a generic word like "sibling." Your older brother is your *gēge* (哥哥), your younger brother is your *dìdi* (弟弟), your older sister is your *jiějie* (姐姐), and your younger sister is your *mèimei* (妹妹).

Based on these terms, your older male cousin who is the son of your father's brother is your *tánggē* (堂哥), which literally means "ancestral hall older brother," since for your entire lives you will traditionally make sacrifices together to your ancestors in the ancestral hall in your family compound. Similarly, your younger male cousin who is the son of your father's brother is your *tángdì* (堂弟), which literally means "ancestral hall younger brother." Your older female cousin who is the daughter of your father's brother is your *tángjiě* (堂姐), or "ancestral hall older sister," and your younger female cousin who is the daughter of your father's brother is your *tángmèi* (堂妹).

For your cousins who are either the children of your father's sisters, or children of your mother's brothers or sisters, there are separate terms that make it clear that they do not grow up or live in the same family compound with you. All four of these terms use the prefix 表 (*biǎo*), meaning "outer," and use the words for "older brother," "younger brother," "older sister," or "younger sister" as suffixes to indicate their gender and age relative to you. Therefore, if those cousins are older than you and male, they are your *biǎogē* (表哥); if younger than you and male they are your *biǎodì* (表弟); if older than you and female they are your *biǎojiě* (表姐); and if younger than you and female they are your *biǎomèi* (表妹).

There are even specific terms for your great-grandparents, great-great-grandparents, etc., for each side of the family, dating back as much as ten generations. Every culture places a high value on family as the foundation of its society, but arguably no other society so carefully describes each and every family relationship with a special and distinct term as does that of China.

21

• •

Holidays

By far the most important holiday on the Chinese calendar is the Chinese New Year. It's as if we in the U.S. celebrated an extended holiday from Thanksgiving through our New Year's Day, as a vacation time to be reunited with our families. Most people in the West have heard about Chinese New Year, but few know about the other six major holidays that people in mainland China celebrate each year: the Lantern Festival on the fifteenth day of the New Year; the Qingming (Tomb Sweeping/Memorial Day) Festival in early spring; International Workers Day (Labor Day) on May 1; the Dragon Boat Festival in early summer; the Mid-Autumn Day Festival in early fall; and National Day on October 1.

These are the seven public holidays, but other traditional festivals are observed as well. People in China use the solar

calendar for daily life, just as we do in the West, but their traditional holidays are observed according to the lunar calendar that was in use when these festivals were established in ancient times. All but two of the seven public holidays are observed according to the lunar rather than the solar calendar. Therefore even though January 1 is considered the beginning of the year, Chinese New Year is celebrated on the first day of the first lunar month. That results in the Chinese New Year starting any time between the middle of January and the middle of February, depending on how the lunar and solar calendars line up in any particular year.

The New Year celebration always includes a family reunion dinner on New Year's Eve. Fish is usually served, since the word for "fish," 鱼 (*yú*), is a homophone with the word for "surplus" or "abundance," 余 (*yú*). The hope is that the family will have abundance every year. In the north it is also customary to eat 饺子 (*jiǎozi*), Chinese ravioli. *Jiaozi* were traditionally eaten starting at midnight when the old year transitions into the new, based on the word 交 (*jiāo*), meaning to "join" or "meet," a homophone with the *jiǎo* in *jiǎozi*. At midnight fireworks are set off, a tradition that predates the Fourth of July fireworks in the U.S. by a great many centuries.

The New Year holiday is not only a time to spend with

family, but is also when Chinese are expected to pay a visit to their relatives. Parents and other older relatives traditionally give children red envelopes with money inside as a New Year's present. Families post poetic couplets on red paper on either side of their front doors that express wishes for the family to prosper in the New Year.

It is also customary to post the character for "good fortune," 福, on the middle of the door to the home, in the hope of bringing good luck to the household in the coming year.

Officially the Chinese are only given three days off to celebrate the New Year, but many work units "borrow" the previous week's two weekend days together with the two days of the following weekend to give their employees a seven-day vacation. All schools including universities take approximately a month off, from around the middle of January until the middle of February. China has close to three hundred million migrant workers who have come to the large cities from the countryside or from smaller, less developed cities to find better paying work than in their home provinces. These migrant workers account for over a third of the nation's workforce. The New Year holiday is one of only two times in the year when these workers can return home to see their parents as well as any children they've left behind in their native villages and towns. The result is the greatest annual migration of people in the world, as hundreds of millions of Chinese travel home to visit their families.

During the New Year holiday one of the most prominent activities is the staging of a lion or dragon dance in the main parks of the larger cities or in the main squares of smaller towns and in the countryside. That tradition can also be seen in the Chinatowns in cities across the U.S. and Canada.

A second traditional holiday, which falls on the fifteenth day of the first lunar month, is the Yuanxiao Festival, popularly known as the "Lantern Festival." On this day homes and places of business put up lanterns in a great variety of designs. These now use electric bulbs, but traditionally children were given paper lanterns with candles inside to carry through the streets on the night of the festival. Since the moon is always full on the fifteenth day of a lunar month, people customarily eat glutinous rice balls stuffed with red bean paste to symbolize the moon.

The next traditional holiday on the calendar is the Qingming Festival, popularly called the "Tomb-Sweeping Festival." It falls every year on the fifteenth day of the spring equinox, just when the weather begins to turn warmer. Similar to Memorial Day in the U.S., this is traditionally a time for people to commemorate their ancestors by visiting their graves. They sweep the tombs; lay willow branches, flowers, or plastic plants on the graves; leave offerings of food, tea, or wine for the spirits of their ancestors to enjoy; and burn paper money for them to use in the afterlife. They pray in front of the graves and entreat their ancestors to bless their families. This custom dates back over 2,500 years to the ancient Zhou dynasty.

Since this holiday comes just after the spring equinox, when things are beginning to turn green in the north and flowers are already blooming in the south, the Chinese people will use this as an opportunity for a spring outing. One tradition, dating back well over a thousand years to the Tang dynasty, is to fly kites. What makes kite flying during the Qingming Festival special is that the kites are flown in the evening as well as during the day. Little colored lanterns are tied to the kites themselves or to the strings holding the kites. When flown at night, the kites are said to resemble twinkling stars.

The fourth major traditional holiday in China is the Duanwu or "Double Fifth" Festival, popularly known as the "Dragon Boat Festival." It occurs on the fifth day of the fifth lunar month. This festival dates back over two thousand years and is commonly said to commemorate the ancient Chinese official and poet Qu Yuan (340–278 BC). Qu Yuan served in a high position at the court of the king of Chu during the Warring States period. When he opposed the decision of the king to ally himself with the increasingly powerful state of Qin, Qu was banished and even accused of treason. In exile, Qu Yuan wrote a great deal of poetry, including the famous long poem "Li Sao" ("Encountering Sorrow"). In his twenty-eighth year in exile Qu Yuan learned that his native kingdom of Chu had been captured by the king of Qin. In deep despair, Qu Yuan committed suicide by drowning himself in the Miluo River.

Legend has it that the local people, who admired Qu Yuan, raced out in their boats to save him, or at least to retrieve his body. This is the supposed origin of the dragon boat races that take place all across China and Taiwan. These competitions have taken place annually for more than two thousand years as part of religious ceremonies and folk customs, but in modern times, beginning in Hong Kong in 1976, dragon boat racing has become an international sport. The wooden boats used for these events usually are decorated with dragon heads at the bow and dragon tails in the stern. Large boats are rowed by eighteen to twenty men, with eight to ten in the smaller boats, not including the helmsman and the drummer who dictate the speed of the rowing.

During this holiday the Chinese eat *zongzi*. These are balls of sticky rice, ranging in shape from an elongated cone in northern China to a tetrahedron shape in the south. Stuffed with fillings that vary from sweet red bean paste or taro in the north to the duck eggs and pork favored in the south, the *zongzi* are wrapped in bamboo leaves, reed leaves, or other large flat leaves and then boiled or steamed. This tradition stems from the legend that when Qu Yuan's body could not be found in the water after he drowned himself, the local people dropped balls of sweet rice into the river so that the fish would eat them and not disturb the body of the dead poet.

The traditional Chinese Valentine's Day falls on the seventh day of the lunar month and is, therefore, known as the Qi Xi ("Seventh Night") Festival. Dating back over two millennia, the holiday is based on the legend of a young cowherd who met and fell in love with a beautiful girl he saw weaving. Not realizing that the weaving maid was really the seventh daughter of the Goddess of Heaven come down to earth to enjoy a more exciting life, the cowherd married the girl without the knowledge of the goddess. They lived happily for some time and had two children together. When the goddess finally learned of this, she turned the two lovers into the stars Altair and Vega and created the Milky Way to separate the two on either end. Out of pity for these literally star-crossed lovers, once a year the magpies of the world fly up into the sky to form a bridge for the lovers to be together for that one night.

In today's China young couples celebrate this holiday by exchanging presents such as chocolate and flowers and by going out to dinner together, much as Valentine's Day is celebrated in the U.S. Unlike our Valentine's Day, however, some Chinese couples may float paper lanterns on a river and pray that their love will last forever. Many Chinese choose to get engaged or married on this day. In larger cities all over the country matchmaking events take place, where many parents can be found posting information about their adult children in the hope of finding them a potential spouse.

Another traditional holiday observed in China is the Mid-Autumn Festival. This occurs on the fifteenth day of the eighth month in the lunar calendar, generally sometime in September. This festival was created as far back as the Shang dynasty more than three thousand years ago, to give thanks for the harvest when the first moon of autumn was full. This is the other major time of year for family reunions in China, in addition to the Chinese New Year. When family members live in places far from one another, they can always look up at the full moon knowing that their loved ones are gazing at the same moon and thinking about them.

When the Chinese look at the moon they don't see a man in the moon, the way Americans traditionally do, but instead are reminded of the famous ancient legend of the beautiful Chang'e, who accidentally took the elixir of immortality and flew to the moon. Here she is said to remain, with a jade rabbit as her only companion. When the Chinese in 2007 launched its first lunar probe, the robotic spacecraft was named after Chang'e. So, too, was the second unmanned probe in 2010. When a third Chang'e spacecraft landed on the moon in 2013, making China only the third country in the world to achieve such a feat, it delivered the robotic rover Yutu ("Jade Rabbit") covered in gold foil to the lunar surface.

During this holiday it is traditional to eat "moon cakes." These are round pastries with a stuffing that varies from region to region to include sweet bean paste, lotus seed paste, or nuts in the north to egg yolks, duck, and roast pork in the south. The round cakes represent the full moon, which symbolizes family harmony and unity. This is another Chinese festival featuring colorful lanterns. In southern China it is common to see performances of "dragon dances" and "lion dances" just as during the Chinese New Year.

The last major holiday of the year is National Day on October 1. This commemorates the founding of the People's Republic on that date in 1949, just as July 4 is the day when Americans celebrate the founding of their country.

A military parade and celebration are held in Tiananmen Square in the heart of Beijing on October 1. Most work units and all schools are officially given three days off, but they combine it with weekends to create a longer vacation from

October 1 through 7 that is nowadays referred to as "Golden Week." This has become a major time for Chinese to travel across the country and abroad.

22

The Chinese Written Language

To those who have never studied Chinese, its written language must look impenetrable and almost impossible to learn. But that's obviously just appearances. The literacy rate in China today is now close to 100% for young adults 15 to 24. And the Japanese, who use over two thousand Chinese characters in their written language, have an almost 100% literacy rate for their entire population. The Chinese writing system is actually a rather ingenious system of pictographs that has helped it survive as the only system of picture writing left in the world today. The only other pictograph language in existence after the time of Christ, Egyptian hieroglyphics, fell into disuse around 1,800 years ago.

Every Chinese character contains at least one "radical," i.e., root part, a simple picture that helps to show the general meaning of that character. For example, the "water" radical, written as 水, usually abbreviated and placed on the left side of a character, is found in all words that are either bodies of water (河 "river"; 湖 "lake") or that have something to do with water, such as the character for "thirsty," written as 渴. The "tree" radical is found in all characters that are either names of trees (松 "pine"; 李 "plum tree"), or in words for things made of wood (床 "bed"; 椅 "chair"). The radical is often found on the left side of a character, but sometimes appears on the right side, the top, or the bottom. Although there are 214 radicals in all, 40 of the radicals are found in three-quarters of all Chinese characters. And the most commonly used 100 account for nearly 99% of all characters.

One popular misconception is that there is no correspondence between the Chinese spoken and written language. In fact, approximately 90% of Chinese characters currently in use also contain another type of pictograph that gives a hint to the pronunciation of the character. These are called "phonetics." They are often characters by themselves but are written as parts of more complex characters as a pronunciation clue. For example, in the character for "ocean," written as 洋, the "water" radical is on the left side, signifying that the character has to do with water. The right side has the character for "sheep," written as 羊, as the phonetic, since the word for "sheep," *yáng*, is pronounced the same as the word for "ocean," *yáng*.

Part of the brilliance of the Chinese written language is that phonetics often contribute to the meaning of a character, as well as give a clue as to pronunciation. For example, in the character 忘 *wàng*, "to forget," the "heart" radical 心 is on the bottom of the character, indicating that the character has to do with emotions or thought. The top part has the character for "death," 亡 *wáng*, as the phonetic. In addition to serving as a clue to pronunciation, this particular character was chosen as a phonetic for its metaphorical value: to forget something is literally to have a thought die in the heart or mind.

Many Chinese characters exist in two different versions. Chinese in Taiwan and Hong Kong as well as those in the U.S. and Canada continue to use the "traditional" form of the characters as they have been written for the past several millennia. In the 1950s the Chinese in mainland China began using "simplified" forms of many of the characters in order to promote literacy. Most students of the Chinese language in the U.S. and Canada only learn these simplified versions of the characters, since they are the ones used by the more than 1.4 billion people living in mainland China.

The traditional and simplified versions of the Chinese written language are not that different from one another. Only a relatively small percentage of characters were simplified, and these are often just the same shorthand versions of those characters already in use in previous centuries. To promote literacy, all the Chinese government did was make those versions the "official" way to write them.

Very often it was the "radicals" that were simplified. For example, the "speech" radical on the left side of characters was simplified, so that the word to "say" is no longer written in mainland China as 說 but rather as 说. The "metal" radical on the left side of characters for various metals or things made of metal was also simplified, so that the word for "silver," for example, is no longer written as 銀 but rather as 银.

When characters were simplified, it was done in one of three ways. The most common was to only write a barebones, skeletal outline of the original character. For example, the pictograph for "horse," traditionally written as 馬, is now written as 马. The pictograph for "east," 東, which shows the sun (日) rising above the trees (木) in the east, is now written as 东.

A second way in which some characters were simplified was by eliminating the phonetic for the most common character written with a particular radical. For example, the character for "spacious; broad," 廣, is the most common character that uses the radical 广. The simplified version of the character eliminated the phonetic clue 黃 ("yellow") and is thus written in mainland China and Singapore simply as 广.

The third and least common way that some characters

狗	龍	馬	猴
DOG	DRAGON	HORSE	MONKEY
牛	猪	兔	羊
OX	PIG	RABBIT	RAM
鼠	鷄	蛇	虎
RAT	ROOSTER	SNAKE	TIGER

were simplified was by creating a completely new character to replace the traditional one. For example, the old character "listen; hear," 聽, a particularly complicated one, was replaced with 听, written with the "mouth" radical (口) on the left, referring to listening to something that someone else says, with the phonetic clue on the right given as 斤 ("axe").

A lot of people are afraid to tackle Chinese because they fear there are just too many thousands of individual characters to learn. They may have heard that there are some older dictionaries that contain nearly fifty thousand different single characters. However, most of these characters are very rare, and they include many ancient and obscure characters that are now almost never used. The number of characters commonly used by the Chinese in the present day is a great many times fewer than that figure of fifty thousand.

If you are familiar with the five hundred most common characters in Chinese you can read approximately 75% of anything written in modern Chinese. If you know a thousand characters, you can read close to 90% of everything written in Chinese today. A knowledge of two thousand characters will allow you to read all but around 3% of all written materials. High school graduates in China today know close to three thousand characters, sufficient for them to read pretty much anything written in modern Chinese. The rapidly growing number of Chinese university graduates know a lot more than three thousand characters, however.

China's amazingly rapid economic growth in the past four decades has been accompanied by an impressive improvement in the literacy rate. In 1990 the literacy rate was only 78%. By 2010 it had risen to 95%, and it continues to improve. China still has a way to go to match the nearly 100% literacy rate in advanced countries like the U.S., of course. Nevertheless that China's young people between the ages of fifteen and twenty-four have a literacy rate of 99.6% makes it evident that in the coming decades China will attain the same rate of literacy as the most developed nations in the world.

23

The Chinese Spoken Language

When English native speakers hear Chinese spoken, it must seem a most incomprehensible language. There are virtually no cognates with English, as there are with other Western languages. And Chinese is a tonal language; that is, the intonation of a word changes its meaning. Just as the written language seems impossible for a non-native speaker to learn, so too does the spoken language.

The Chinese spoken language is actually not that difficult to learn. For one thing, there are no difficult rules of conjugation to master as in Western languages. Instead of saying "I see, you see, he/she sees" the Chinese say the equivalent of "I see, you see, he/she see," with the same word *tā* meaning both "he" and "she" as well as "him" and "her." Because there is no conjugation, there is no use of tense in Chinese either. Instead of saying, "I saw her yesterday" the Chinese simply say, "I yesterday see she." Since we're talking about yesterday, it's obvious that we're talking about something that happened in the past.

There is no declension in the Chinese language either. Instead of saying "I see her; she sees me," the Chinese simply say the equivalent of "I see she; she see I."

Chinese also has no genders. There is no need to learn the difference between *la muchacha bonita* and *el muchacho bonito*, as in Spanish, for example. Romance languages have two genders, but German and Russian have as many as three. The word "girl" in German (*Mädchen*) is neuter and thus must be preceded by the article *das* when saying "the girl" (*das Mädchen*). But the word "table" (*Tafel*) is feminine, and therefore is proceeded by the article *die* when saying "the table" (*die Tafel*). Chinese has no such genders to worry about.

Chinese also lacks plurals. Non-native speakers of English have to learn that in English we say "one house, two houses" but "one mouse, two mice." The Chinese language considers plurals unnecessary. In Chinese we simply say the English equivalent of "one house, two house" or "one mouse, two mouse." It's obvious to the listener or reader in Chinese that there is a plurality of whatever noun is being mentioned, simply by seeing or hearing the number that precedes it.

It's true that Chinese is very different from Western

languages in that it is a tonal language. That means that you must make your voice go up or down to change the meaning of a word. Mandarin Chinese, the dialect that has been the "national language" for many centuries, fortunately only has four different tones. Each word has one of those tones. (It was fortunate for learners of Chinese that the Cantonese dialect, with its six different tones, did not become the national language!)

It happens that the national language of China and Taiwan, Mandarin, has the same four tones or intonations as in English:

First tone	high, level tone
Second tone	rising tone
Third tone	downward before rising up
Fourth tone	sharp downward tone

The difference is that how we intone a word in English doesn't completely change the definition of the word, only the feeling behind it. Consider the sound "oh" for example. If we say the word "oh" with a high, level pitch, sustaining it for a second or two, as in "ooohhh, that's great!" we have the "first tone" in Chinese. This can be indicated by a tone mark, which is a line running over the vowel of the word, or by a number in parentheses immediately following the word.

If we say the same sound "oh" with a rising intonation, as if we're asking the question "oh, is that so?" then we have the second tone in Mandarin Chinese.

If we offer sympathy to someone by saying "oh" with a falling intonation but with our voice rising back up at the end, as in "oh, that's too bad," we have the third tone in Chinese.

Finally if we say "oh" with our voice starting fairly high up and falling, as in "oh, that's cool," we have the fourth and final tone of Chinese.

When you learn a word in Chinese you do have to learn the correct tone, or you could be in big trouble. Unlike in English, when you change the tone of a word in Chinese, it completely changes the dictionary definition of a word as well as the "character" or "pictograph" with which it's written.

Here are some examples of the difference a tone can make to a word.

Let's take the often-used example of the sound "ma." Now in almost every language of the world "ma" means "mother." It does in Chinese, too, but only if you pronounce "ma" with the first or "high, level tone." If you say "ma" with the second or "rising" tone, it means "hemp; marijuana"! If you say it with the third tone, "ma" means "horse." And if you say "ma" with the fourth or "falling" tone, then you've changed the meaning once again, this time to "curse; scold; yell at."

Therefore the sentence *mā mà mǎ* means "Mom yelled at the horse." However, since there are no tenses or plurals in Chinese, that simple sentence could also possibly mean "Mom yelled at the horses," "Mom yells at the horse," or "Mom yells at horses," depending on the context.

Here's another example of the importance of saying the tones correctly. A young American was studying elementary Chinese with a lovely young Chinese woman. He says: "Wo yao wen ni" (I want to ask you), but he's not sure of the tone for the word *wen*, which means "to ask." So he tries the second tone and says: "Wǒ yào wén nǐ." Unfortunately *wén* with the second tone means "to smell," so what he said was "I want to sniff you." The young woman shakes her head puzzled. The young man realizes that he's said the tone wrong and tries another tone instead. This time he says emphatically: "Wǒ yào wěn nǐ "(I want to kiss you). *Wěn* with the third tone means "to kiss." The young woman is about to leave the room. Finally in desperation the young man shouts out: "Wǒ yào wèn nǐ." Ah, the fourth tone did it. "What do you want to ask me?" the young woman finally replies, much relieved.

Yao Ming was a celebrated Chinese basketball player from Shanghai who was the all-star center for the Houston Rockets many years ago. His name is pronounced as "Yáo Míng," with both words said with the second or "rising" tone.

However, American TV commentators persisted in saying his name with the fourth tone as Yào Mìng, in the emphatic way we tend to pronounce names in English. This was really laughable to Chinese speakers, since *yào mìng* literally means "to kill someone or drive them to their death," or alternately to describe something that's a nuisance. It's also often used as a suffix on adjectives to mean "terribly ..."!

If Chinese is so simple, then why don't all Americans pick it up as fast as they learn to use a cell phone? One factor is that there are almost no cognates between Chinese and English. That is to say that there are very few words in Chinese that sound like their equivalent in English. Because of their common Latin roots around 60% of words in French or Spanish have words that sound somewhat similar to the word with the same meaning in English. German and Dutch have around 25% of cognates with English, which isn't surprising given that English is really a Germanic language. Chinese, on the other hand, has only a little over a hundred words that derive from English. Most of those are for various Western foods or beverages, and even with those the pronunciation is distorted enough to be difficult to recognize.

For example, the Chinese word for hamburger is *hàn-bǎobǎo* ("hahn-bow-bow," with the "bow" pronounced as in "to bow before a king"). Coca-Cola is *kěkǒukělè* ("kuh-koh-kuh-luh" = "pleases mouth, can have joy"). But most Chinese words do not sound at all like their English counterpart. The word for "computer" is *diàn nǎo* ("dien-now"), literally, "electric brain." To learn Chinese, you have to forget about getting any help from English or French or German. You need to learn to make some strange sounds that will be totally unfamiliar to you.

Given how simple Chinese grammar is compared to the much more complex grammars of Western languages, and that Chinese words are very short, either just one or two syllables, it is not impossible at all for foreigners to learn to speak at least some Chinese. In a globalizing world in which Chinese is by far the most commonly spoken language on the planet and in which the U.S. and China are increasingly interconnected, for Americans and other English speakers to learn Chinese has great value.

Finally, one of the particular joys of speaking Chinese with Chinese people is to experience their delight that a foreigner can say anything at all in their language beyond *nǐ hǎo*, meaning "hello." As a foreign tourist in Paris or Berlin you have to speak French or German very well indeed to impress the natives. But in China you get big strokes as a foreigner just for being able to say a few phrases in Chinese. Chinese is so different from Western languages that few Westerners ever bother to learn even one word of it.

24

Chinese Dialects

As the number of Chinese language programs including Chinese immersion programs continues to increase in schools across the U.S., many Americans have become aware that the main dialect of Chinese spoken in China is Mandarin. However, most Americans are confused by the nature of Chinese dialects, and many continue to believe that Cantonese is almost as important a dialect as Mandarin.

Mandarin is the national language of China, as well as of Taiwan, and along with English it is one of the two national languages of Singapore. It is the dialect of Chinese spoken at home by approximately two-thirds of the Chinese population. It's never been known in Chinese as "Mandarin." That English term was given it by Westerners in the 19th century, because it was the language spoken by the *dà rén* (major officials) of the Manchus who ruled China at the time.

In former centuries Mandarin was called in Chinese *guānhuà*, or "official language," since it was the lingua franca of all government officials in the Qing dynasty (1644–1912). Mandarin is now called *pǔtōnghuà* ("common talk") in mainland China and *guóyǔ* ("national language") in Taiwan. It is taught in all the schools in China and Taiwan and is the principal dialect used for TV and radio programs.

The Chinese spoken language in general is called either *hànyǔ* ("language of the Han Chinese") or *zhōngguó-huà* ("Middle Kingdom talk"). There are seven major dialects of the spoken language. Mandarin is by far the most commonly spoken at home and is used as the common language for all the people in China and Taiwan. Mandarin is the only language spoken by over 70% of the population in China, with variations of Mandarin spoken in northern and southwestern China. A sub-dialect of Mandarin called Jin is spoken in Shanxi Province as well as in parts of Shaanxi, Hebei, Henan, and Inner Mongolia.

If all those speakers are included, Mandarin speakers may be said to make up as much as 75% of all Chinese speakers.

The second most common dialect is not Cantonese, but the Wu dialect.

This is the dialect spoken in the provinces of Jiangsu

and Zhejiang, including the huge city of Shanghai, by around eighty million native speakers, or close to 7% of all Chinese in mainland China. Although that is not an insignificant percentage of the population, it is nevertheless ten to eleven times fewer than Mandarin's. And the speakers of the Wu dialect also need to learn Mandarin to be able to converse with Chinese people from the rest of China.

The third most commonly spoken dialect is Yue, which we refer to as Cantonese in English, since it is the major dialect of the province of Canton, or Guǎngdōng in Mandarin. Yue, or Cantonese, is the native dialect of more than 6% of the Chinese people, including those in Hong Kong and Macau. The reason that many Americans wrongly believe Cantonese to be as important a dialect as Mandarin is that almost all the early immigrants to the U.S. in the 19th century were from the province of Canton. It was mostly the Chinese from this coastal province, which includes the international port of Hong Kong, who helped build the railroads in the American West and who until recently populated the Chinatowns in the U.S. and Canada.

The fourth most commonly spoken dialect is Min or Fukkienese, variations of which are spoken in the southeastern province of Fujian as well as on Hainan Island. There are around fifty million native speakers of this dialect, comprising approximately 5% of all Chinese speakers in mainland China. Min is also the principal Chinese dialect spoken in Taiwan.

Other dialects include Xiang, or Hunanese, spoken by the people of Hunan Province, with around 3% of Chinese speakers; Hakka, spoken by the Hakka people who live in several provinces in southern China, comprising around 2.5% of Chinese speakers; and Gan, spoken in Jiangxi Province, accounting for approximately 2% of speakers.

The seven different dialects of Chinese are mutually unintelligible. The difference between the various Chinese dialects is arguably even greater than that between the Romance languages. If they did not share a common written form and if China were not a unified country, most linguists would consider them to be separate languages.

That is even true of many of the subdialects of both Cantonese and Fukkienese. As a result, people in one county or village may not understand the speech of those living in nearby counties or villages. Fortunately Mandarin, as the national language, allows almost all Chinese to be able to communicate with one another all across China.

25

Chinese Surnames

China has over 1.4 billion people, and 50 million Chinese live outside of mainland China, but there are only around two hundred common surnames for 91.5% of these ethnically Chinese populations. Thousands of surnames have been recorded in Chinese history, but most have either vanished or been simplified. Currently there are only a little over three thousand surnames used, the great majority of which are fairly uncommon.

Some statistics: The top two hundred family names account for as many as 96% of the Chinese people in the mainland, with another five hundred names comprising the remaining 4%. Between mainland China and Taiwan, nineteen family names cover as much as 55.6% of all ethnic Chinese, and the top one hundred names include almost 85% of all family names. The most common fifty surnames are estimated to make up 70% of all Chinese people in the world. These figures certainly affirm the term in Chinese for "the common people," namely 老百姓 (*lǎobǎixìng*), which literally means "the old hundred surnames."

As astonishing as the relatively small number of surnames for Chinese people may be, it can't compare with the even smaller number of family names for Koreans. Around 20% of the forty-nine million people of South Korea have the family name Kim. The second most common last name is Lee, and Park (or Pak) is the third. The three last names combined cover around 45% of all Koreans!

By contrast, there are more than six million last names in the United States, which has always been a nation of immigrants from all over the world.

The ten most common surnames in mainland China are Li (李), Wang (王), Zhang (张), Liu (刘), Chen (陈), Yang (杨), Huang (黄), Zhao (赵), Wu (吴), and Zhou (周). More than 275 million people share one of the three most common surnames of Li, Wang, and Zhang in mainland China alone, approximately a fifth of the entire population. There are nearly 100 million Chinese just with the surname Li. More people in China have those three most common Chinese surnames than there are people in Indonesia, the world's fourth most populous country!

Most Chinese family names have only one character. There are about twenty family names made up of two characters, including Sima (司马), Ouyang (欧阳), Zhuge (诸葛), and Situ (司徒).

The characters used to write the various surnames generally have meaning, just as surnames in English and other European languages commonly do. For example, 李 (Li) means "plum." 王 (Wang) means "king"; those who originally had this surname were descendants of the royal families of the Shang and Zhou dynasties (approximately 1766–1046 BC and 1046–256 BC). 张 (Zhang) means "extend; expand." The character is written with a picture of a bow on the left side (弓). This surname was originally bestowed upon the Supervisor of the Bow and Arrow Makers for the kings of the Shang and Zhou dynasties. The last name 马 (Ma) means "horse." 杨 (Yang) means "willow tree." 黄 (Huang) means "yellow." And 白 (Bai) means "white."

Surnames are not evenly distributed across China. In northern China, Wáng (王) is the most common surname and is shared by close to 10% of the population. Lǐ (李), Zhāng (张), and Liú (刘) are the other most common family names in the north. In the south of China, Chén (陈) is the most common, accounting for well over 10% of the population, followed by Lǐ (李), Huáng (黄), Lín (林), and Zhāng (张).

Because the Chinese language does not use an alphabet, transliterating Chinese names into foreign languages such as English creates a number of problems. Chinese surnames may be shared by people who speak different dialects and thus may have different pronunciations of their surnames. As a result, it is common for the same surname to be transliterated differently. For instance, the family name Wang is romanized as Wong by Cantonese speakers in the U.S. and Canada.

To complicate matters, the Chinese in Taiwan use a different form of romanized Chinese than that used by Chinese in the mainland. The last name Zhang (张), as transliterated by mainlanders, is rendered as Chang by Taiwanese in the U.S. and Canada. What makes this particularly confusing is that there is also a last name Chang (长) as written by mainland Chinese in the West, but as Ch'ang when written by a Taiwanese. The last name Zhou (周) as transliterated by Chinese from the mainland, is written as Chou by Taiwanese in the U.S. and Canada.

26

Chinese Names in Western Media

Anyone who can speak even a little Chinese is irked by the failure of TV and radio announcers to come close to pronouncing Chinese names and words correctly, even on stations like NPR or the BBC. During the 2012 coverage of the Olympics, the sixteen-year-old Chinese girl who won two gold medals in swimming, Ye ShiWen, was falsely accused of doping by the coach of the American swim team. As TV and radio commentators reported on this for many days, they all referred to her over and over again as "Yay She-When." They never bothered to check with the multitude of Chinese speakers available to them as consultants to discover that the name of this young woman is actually pronounced "Yeh Sure-When."

Qiu Bo, who received a silver medal in the 2012 Olympics in platform diving, was called "Kyuu Boh." That's a far cry from the way his name is actually pronounced, namely "Chioh Bwoh." And the Chinese woman boxer, Ren Cancan, had her first name butchered as "Can Can," like the boisterous dance made famous by Jacques Offenbach's music and the Moulin Rouge. It was difficult for Chinese speakers in the U.S. to realize the commentators were referring to a woman whose name is pronounced close to "Ren Tsahn-Tsahn."

During those same Olympics, the NBC commentators, as well as those on BBC radio and NPR, hardly ever pronounced the name of a single Chinese athlete correctly. That was in

spite of the fact that the Chinese won the second most medals of any country and many of its athletes were known to be
the leading contenders for gold. The TV and radio stations
did not think it important enough to check how the names of
these world-class athletes are actually pronounced.

It was no different at the 2008 Olympics in Beijing. Al
Roker, from the NBC *Today* show, introduced one Chinese
word or phrase each day during the Olympics. He stood there
in front of Olympic Stadium, surrounded by a large crowd of
Chinese people, and butchered every word he was supposedly trying to teach all of America. Neither he nor the NBC
staff ever thought to check with any of the hundreds of native
speakers of Chinese gathered there to find out how those
basic Chinese words and phrases are really pronounced.

This lack of even a small attempt to try to pronounce
Chinese names and words correctly is not malicious by any
means. It does, however, convey a lack of respect and care
when it comes to the most commonly spoken language in the
world and the national language of the world's most populous
nation.

Two critically important Chinese words that are almost
always pronounced incorrectly here in the U.S., including
by newscasters, are the words "Beijing" and "yuan." The "j"
in the name of China's capital city is not pronounced with
the soft "j" sound used in French, such as in the phrase "Je
suis." The Chinese language lacks that sound entirely. The "j"
in "Beijing" is pronounced like the "j" in "jingle." So when
TV and radio broadcasters pronounce the capital of the biggest nation in the world with a "je" sound, it is like Chinese
announcers calling the U.S. capital "Wachington Dee Shee."

The Chinese dollar is the yuan. It is not pronounced
"you-anne" or "you-awn," as you so often hear in newscasts
in the U.S. or on the BBC. It is actually pronounced similar to
"you-when," or "U.N.," said quickly as if it were one syllable.

To compound this error, "yuan" is not the real name of the Chinese currency, which is, rather, "Renminbi" or RMB, as anyone who ever has exchanged money in China well knows.

To be fair, the way Chinese names and words are spelled in transliterated English is more than a bit misleading. Chinese is the one language in the world that is entirely comprised of pictographs or "characters" and lacks any alphabet or syllabary. When the Chinese government in the 1950s wished to create a romanized transliteration of their language to make it easier for their young children as well as foreigners to learn, a system called "pinyin" was invented. That system of romanized Chinese is now used all around the world except in Taiwan. Pinyin was not created for the sake of English speakers, however, so it takes five or ten minutes to learn how to pronounce the sounds of Chinese when they are spelled using the Roman alphabet.

There are five consonant sounds whose spelling in pinyin misleads English speakers. A "q" is pronounced as "ch" when followed by an "i" or a "u." An "x" is said like an "sy," as in the Spanish word "sierra" (as in the Sierra Nevadas). A "zh" is pronounced with a "j" sound, when followed by any vowel other than "i," in which case the "j" sound is simply spelled with a "j." A "z" is pronounced as "dz," similar to the sound at the end of the English word "ads." Finally, a "c," as in Ren CanCan's name, is pronounced with a "ts" sound, as in the final sound in the English word "its."

Tricky vowel combinations that throw off English-language broadcasters include "iu," pronounced as "ee-oh" rather than "ee-you"; "ui," which is pronounced similar to "way" and not "uu-ee"; and "uan," said like our English word "when," and not "uu-ahn." English-language TV and radio announcers could refer to a simple chart with these hints on pronunciation. Or they could find out the accurate pronunciation of the most basic Chinese names and words from one of the nearly 5 million Chinese who live in the U.S., or one of the nearly 160,000 college students from mainland China studying at American colleges and universities, or one of the 60,000 American college students learning Chinese.

Another problem that plagues English speakers when they encounter a Chinese name is the fact that in China, as in most East Asian countries, a person's surname, or family name, is usually said first, followed by the given name. In the West we have become accustomed to seeing many Japanese names run in the familiar "Westernized" first-name, last-name convention, such as Akira Kurosawa or Toshiro Mifune, when in Japan itself it would be Kurosawa Akira or Mifune Toshiro. The baseball player, known in his own country as Suzuki Ichirō, is always called Ichiro Suzuki, or simply Ichiro, in the U.S. A lot of Westerners still don't realize that Chinese basketball superstar Yao Ming's surname is Yao.

Most Chinese still use three characters in their name: The surname is one character and the given name is two characters. There are rare two-character surnames, such as Ouyang (Ohyang) and Szto (Sigh-toe), and these are usually found in the south of China. A man who is called Li GuoMing is Mr. Li, and not Mr. Guoming or Mr. Ming. When romanized, the given name is usually written as a single word, which is an immediate clue that Li is, in fact, the surname here. To confuse things a bit, these days some Chinese who are aware of overseas customs when meeting foreigners will give their name in the Western fashion, with their given name first. In these instances it is best to ask them for clarification as to which is their surname.

27

● ●

Sayings You Thought Were Chinese . . . But Aren't

When people in English-speaking countries came to realize the great variety and profundity of Chinese proverbs, they began to collect them. Often the translations into English of these very pithy Chinese sayings were embellished so fancifully that their origin became unrecognizable to the Chinese themselves.

For instance, the saying "the longest journey begins with a single step" is a paraphrase of the old Chinese proverb "a thousand-mile journey begins under your feet." The saying "Give a man a fish and he has fish for a day. Teach a man to fish and he has fish for a lifetime" is actually a loose translation of the Chinese popular saying "Giving a person a fish isn't as good as helping him learn to fish." The maxim "A single spark can set a whole prairie on fire" is also from an ancient Chinese saying.

And the sometimes quoted "One hand alone can't clap; it takes two to quarrel" is derived from a Chinese proverb. However the Chinese version only includes the first half of this saying, even if it does imply the second part.

A great many other sayings are falsely attributed to the Chinese. Although many English speakers firmly believe that the phrase "May you live in interesting times" is an ancient Chinese curse, no one has ever been able to discover its Chinese origin. If someone in the West has invented a Chinese saying or translated it in such a creative way as to be unrecognizable to Chinese people, it ultimately matters little. What matters is that you find in that proverb or saying some truth about life to light your way or lift your heart. The proverbs listed below are particularly popular in the U.S. and are, indeed, quite meaningful. But all have been falsely attributed to the Chinese. Their perspective reflects a Western sensibility, often that of 20th- or 21st-century America, rather than that found in traditional Chinese thought and culture.

Fool me once, shame on you; fool me twice, shame on me.

This quote actually derives from an even older version of an Italian saying quoted by Anthony Weldon in his book *The Court and Character of King James*, published in 1650, which reads "The Italians having a proverb, he that deceives me once, it's his fault; but twice it is my fault." In a 1786 essay by George Horne, an English cleric, is his paraphrase into English of the Italian saying, namely "When a man deceives me once, says the Italian proverb, it is his fault; when twice, it is mine."

Find a job you love and you'll never have to work another day in your life.

This saying is sometimes attributed to the Chinese sage Confucius. Confucius did say, "Isn't it a pleasure to study and practice what you have learned?" But the saying popular in contemporary America is too loose a translation to justify attributing it to China's most famous teacher.

A bird does not sing because it has an answer; it sings because it has a song.

The exact quote, which was also falsely attributed to Maya Angelou on a Forever stamp before the stamp was withdrawn, first appears in the book *A Cup of Sun* by Joan Walsh Anglund, published in 1967.

A book is like a garden carried in one's pocket.
This is actually an old Arabian proverb.

When all you have left is two pennies, buy a loaf of bread with one and a lily with the other.
The Chinese, both past and present, would not think in terms of loaves of bread as a metaphor for food in a culture whose main staples are rice and noodles. The mention of bread is an immediate clue that this proverb could not possibly come from China. It has two possible origins, neither from China. It perhaps derives from a poem by the 13th-century Persian poet, Muslihuddin Sadi, translated into English as

If, of thy mortal goods, thou are bereft,
And from thy slender store two loaves
alone to thee are left,
Sell one and from the dole,
Buy hyacinths to feed the soul.

Another possibility is that it comes from the English poet Elbert Hubbard (1856–1915), who wrote:

If I had but two loaves of bread
I would sell one of them
And buy white hyacinths to feed my soul.

Happiness is not a horse; you cannot harness it.
This is actually a Russian proverb. The Chinese never talk about finding "happiness" as a major goal in life, although Chinese proverbs do mention striving for contentment and tranquility. The pursuit of happiness is one of the principal human objectives expressed in Western thought in recent centuries, but is not something stressed in traditional Asian culture.

Failure is not falling down, but refusing to get up

This is actually a quote from the American author, tel-evangelist, and pastor Robert A. Schuller. Reverend Schuller is the only son of Crystal Cathedral founders Robert H. Schuller and Arvella Schuller, and author of the book *What Happens to Good People When Bad Things Happen*.

28

● ●

Lucky and Unlucky Numbers

The Chinese traditionally believe that certain numbers are lucky and others unlucky, based on those numbers sharing the same pronunciation as certain other words in the Chinese language. A great many Chinese to this day still act on these superstitions.

For example, the number 4 is considered the unluckiest number because the word for "4," 四 (sì), is a homophone with the word "to die," 死 (sǐ), even though it's said with a different tone (inflection). The number 4 is generally avoided in floors of a public building. If you're in an elevator in some hotels and public buildings in southern China and press the button to go to the 50th floor, you may actually only be going to the 36th floor. That's because many buildings in China will omit any floor containing the unlucky number 4.

The number 4 is also avoided in addresses, ID numbers, license plates, and so on, Houses and apartments that have 4 in the address number will sell for much less than ones without. The Chinese will avoid inviting 44 people or 444 people to a wedding. And to give a person a present with the character for "4" on it (四) is tantamount to wishing them dead (死)!

Fortunately the words for most single-digit numbers are considered lucky. The number 8 is considered the luckiest number because the word for "8," 八 (bā), in southern dialects of Chinese is pronounced the same as the word 发 (fā), the first character in the compound word meaning "to become prosperous." Many Chinese, particularly in the southern part of the country, will pay quite a bit extra for phone numbers and license plates that include the number 8 as many times as possible. A man in Hangzhou offered on the Internet to sell his license plate, A8888, for $140,000.

While the Chinese will make a great effort to avoid using the number 4 in daily life, they will try to use 8 whenever they can. In the Beijing Summer Olympics in 2008, the opening ceremony began at 8:08 pm on 8/8/08. Many airlines in Chinese-speaking countries will use combinations of 8 as flight numbers.

Superstitious Chinese think it almost as lucky to have a phone number or license plate that combines the number 1 with the number 8. That's because the character for "1," yī, in certain situations can also be pronounced yāo, a homophone with the word yào, meaning "will." So if your phone number, license plate, home address, hotel room, or whatever is 1818, for example, it sounds to people in southern China like you're saying, "will become wealthy, will become wealthy."

The number 6 is generally considered to be lucky in China because the word for "6," 六 (liù), except for the inflection (tone) sounds like the word in Chinese that means "to flow," 流 (liú). Many businesses display the number 6 to summon good fortune. Whereas in the West the number 666 is by many associated with the devil, multiple sixes are considered lucky by the Chinese, who often say 六六顺 (liù liù shùn), literally, "six six smoothly," implying "things will go smoothly."

The number 9, 九 (*jiǔ*), is also considered a very lucky number. It's not only the highest single digit, but it's also a perfect homophone with the word 久 (*jiǔ*), which means "long lasting/eternal" in Chinese. At birthday parties and at wedding celebrations the number 9 is often featured since it symbolizes longevity. The number 9 was also traditionally associated with the Chinese emperor. The emperor's robes had nine dragons on them, as does a wall in the Forbidden City; and the Forbidden City, the palace of emperors from the 14th through the early 20th centuries, is said to have a total of 9,999½ rooms.

In the Internet age, there are certain combinations of numbers used online as a special shorthand. For example, 88, 八八 (*bā bā*), is often used to say "bye, bye" when signing off. 555, 五五五 (*wǔ wǔ wǔ*), represents the sound of crying, since 5 is a homophone with the onomatopoeic sound of crying 呜呜呜 (*wū wū wū*). 520, 五二〇 (*wǔ èr líng*), is sometimes used as a cute way of saying 我爱你 (*wǒ ài nǐ*), meaning "I love you."

We have mentioned that the number 4 is a taboo number. There are other taboos non-Chinese should be aware of, and most are not related to numbers, although some are. For example, when giving presents to a new friend or a business associate, presenting them in multiples of two suggests good luck and happiness, whereas an odd numbers of gift items is considered unlucky. Don't use white wrapping paper, since white is symbolic of funerals. Taboo gifts include clocks, since the Chinese word for "clock," *zhong* ("jung"), sounds exactly like the word for "the end." Umbrellas also make most inappropriate gifts, since the word for "umbrella" is a homophone for the word that means "separation" or "breaking up." If you present a card along with a present, do not write on it with red ink; red ink is often used when writing a "Dear John" or "Dear Mary" letter to end a relationship. And when you're done eating in China, never place your chopsticks across the top of your bowl or, worse yet, stick them straight up in your rice. The former is just bad manners, but the latter is strictly taboo because it reminds the Chinese of how offerings of vertical incense sticks are traditionally made to the spirits of their dead ancestors—definitely bad form for the dinner table.

29

Dragons in Chinese Folklore

Dragons are featured prominently in Chinese culture, in folklore and as important symbols. Chinese dragons are very different from how we in the West picture those mythical beasts. European dragons are usually depicted as large, fire-breathing, lizard-like creatures that live in caves and are evil and harmful to human beings.

Chinese dragons, on the other hand, are quite different. They are most commonly depicted as snake-like with four legs. Rather than being associated with fire, they are said to have control over water of every kind, including rivers and seas, rain, typhoons, and floods. And instead of being viewed as evil and harmful to people, they are a symbol of power and strength, as well as of good luck and prosperity for people who are worthy of it.

For many centuries the emperors of China used the dragon on their robes and on the walls of their palace as a symbol of their imperial power. The emperor's throne was referred to as the "Dragon Throne." In the Forbidden City, the palace of emperors in Beijing from the mid-1300s until 1911,

there is a famous wall with nine colorful ceramic dragons. The founder of the Han dynasty, Liu Bang, claimed he was born after his mother dreamed of a dragon. There are many Chinese expressions that refer to dragons, most common of all being "hoping one's son will become a dragon," meaning rise to a position of power and success.

The dragon is sometimes used in the West as an emblem or symbol of the nation of China though that is not true in China itself. It was reported that the Chinese government decided not to use the dragon as its official mascot for the 2008 Summer Olympics in Beijing because the dragon is seen as evil in European countries; the government chose cute mascots instead.

In the West there are twelve astrological signs, one for each month, that are believed to determine your personality based on your date of birth. The Chinese also have twelve signs of the zodiac, but they are based on a cycle of twelve years. Each is associated with a certain animal. The dragon is one of them and is considered the luckiest of all the signs to be born under.

Below is the original character for "dragon" as it was written by the Chinese around three thousand years ago.

The right side of the character shows the spiky head of the dragon with claws and a tail. The left side shows it standing upright in all its majesty and power. For the past two thousand years the character has been traditionally written as 龍 as it still is for Chinese people in Taiwan, Hong Kong, the U.S., and Canada, and anywhere else outside of China and Singapore, where in the 1950s it was greatly simplified as 龙.

No matter how it is written, the word for dragon in Mandarin Chinese is pronounced "luhng" (*lóng* in pinyin).

30

Ethnic Groups in China

We in the West tend to think of all the people of China as being Chinese by ethnicity. There are actually fifty-six separate ethnic groups in China. It is true that the Han people, who are ethnically Chinese, do make up between 91% and 92% of the population of China. That leaves over 8% of the Chinese population who are not ethnically Chinese and who belong to one of the other fifty-five ethnic groups in the country. Given that China's population now exceeds 1.4 billion, that means there are well over 100 million people who belong to these minority groups.

The members of these ethnic groups are descendants of societies that were conquered by the Han people in past centuries, so most of them live in the border regions of China. They tend to be concentrated in the more remote areas of the northwest, north, and northeast, as well as in the south and southwest fringes of the country, although large numbers of Han Chinese live in those regions as well.

The major minority ethnic groups are the Zhuang in the southeast mountain areas (over 16 million); the Manchu in the far northeast (around 10.5 million); the indigenous Muslims called the Hui, who are more concentrated in the northwest provinces (nearly 10 million); the Miao in the southeast mountain areas (nearly 9 million); the Turkish minority called the Uyghur, who are largely found in Xinjiang Province or "Chinese Turkestan" in the far northwest (over 8 million); and the Tujia (8 million) and the Yi (nearly 8 million) in the southeast.

There are nearly 6 million Mongols, who mostly live in the Autonomous Region of Inner Mongolia, on the northern Chinese border. Most of the 5.5 million Tibetans live in the Autonomous Region of Tibet on the southwest border of China. While the Mongols have shown little outward resistance to Chinese rule, the unrest and outright protests in Tibet have often captured the attention of human rights watchers in the West, ever since China occupied Tibet by force in 1950. The Turkish minority in Xinjiang, the Uyghur, who are Muslims, are the other major ethnic group that has on occasion held protests to express their dissatisfaction with Chinese rule. After several terrorist attacks by Uyghur separatists in several major cities in China, the Chinese government reacted in late 2018 by arresting hundreds of thousands of Uyghurs and keeping them in what are called re-education camps, which has caused understandable outrage by human rights groups across the world.

The other ethnic minorities in China seem either reasonably content with their lot, or are at least resigned to being ruled by the huge Han majority. The constitution and laws of the People's Republic guarantee equal rights to all ethnic groups in China and help promote economic and cultural development for ethnic minorities. In recent decades the Chinese government has given some special privileges to these minority groups.

One notable preferential treatment ethnic minorities enjoy is that they have not been subject to what we in the West call the "One Child Policy" and may have as many children as they wish. Ethnic minorities are represented in the National People's Congress as well as in governments at the provincial and prefectural levels. Large numbers of ethnic minorities in China live in what are termed "autonomous regions," which comprise nearly two-thirds of the country. These regions guarantee ethnic minorities the freedom to use and teach their ethnic languages and to maintain their own cultural and social customs.

Over eighty languages are used among these ethnic populations, classified into three main groups: (1) the Han, Hui, and Manchu use Mandarin Chinese as their mother tongue; (2) twelve groups use their own language and writing scripts (Mongols, Tibetans, Uyghur, Kazak, and Koreans among them); (3) the remaining groups have a spoken language but not a written script that is in common use. There are five languages printed on all Chinese paper currency: Chinese, Mongolian, Tibetan, Uyghur, and Zhuang.

As suggested above, the Chinese government gives preferential economic development and aid to areas where ethnic minorities live. The majority of the members of these

minorities are farmers and are often exempt from paying any taxes. There is also a kind of "affirmative action" policy for minority students who take the national exams to enter universities in China. If an ethnic minority student manages to obtain even the very minimum score for admission to a prestigious university, the student is eligible for admittance to any of the top Chinese universities. If the minority student scores even fifty points below the minimum for acceptance to any university, he or she is still considered for admission to any of the non-elite schools. There are thirteen universities and institutes in China devoted to the study of minority cultures that enroll about thirty thousand ethnic students. These include the beautiful campus of Guangxi University for Minorities, which has an enrollment of nearly ten thousand students.

Because many of the ethnic minority groups in China have maintained their traditional customs and dress, which seem so much more colorful and exotic than those of the Han majority, they are often featured in TV programs and movies. They are especially prominent on Chinese currency, which often features representatives of the major minority groups in their native dress.

With the "Reform and Opening Up" policy that started in 1980 and increasingly allowed capitalist enterprise, many Han acquired enough money to begin to travel. One of the favorite travel experiences of the wealthier Chinese is to visit minority areas, to see the purportedly exotic rituals of the minority peoples. These minority areas tend to be in beautiful but more remote mountain areas, with some of the most spectacular scenery in China. These include the JiuZhaiGou National Park on the border with Tibet, which contains a number of small Tibetan villages within the park.

Responding to this interest, many minority entrepreneurs are now catering to the Han Chinese tourists by enacting performances similar to what can be seen on Chinese TV, despite perhaps never having grown up practicing the "ethnic" dances, rituals, or songs themselves. In the biggest cities like Beijing and Shanghai are an increasing number of ethnic restaurants where the wait staff are minority youth from their respective provinces who sometimes dress in their traditional ethnic costumes to help attract customers.

In this way, the groups of the various minorities have begun to feel a greater ethnic identity than they might have previously. However, most Chinese minority people do not look, act, or dress much differently from the Han majority. More and more of them have moved out of their native areas, both for work and for schooling, are fluent in Mandarin Chinese, and have assimilated into the general society.

CHINA

Provinces with Major Cities and Capitals

Population

1.415 billion (approx. 18.54% of the world population)

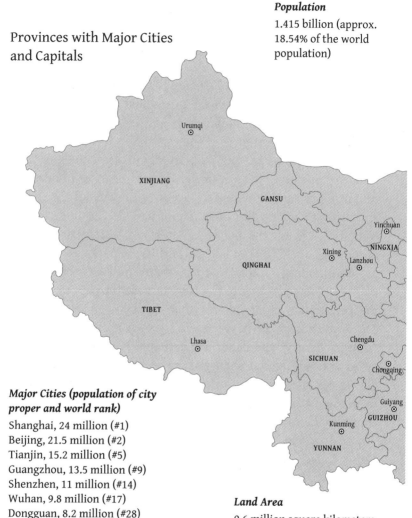

Major Cities (population of city proper and world rank)

Shanghai, 24 million (#1)
Beijing, 21.5 million (#2)
Tianjin, 15.2 million (#5)
Guangzhou, 13.5 million (#9)
Shenzhen, 11 million (#14)
Wuhan, 9.8 million (#17)
Dongguan, 8.2 million (#28)
Chongqing, 8.2 million (#29)
Nanjing, 8.2 million (#30)

Land Area

9.6 million square kilometers (3.7 million square miles)

Major Rivers

Yangtze River, 3,915 miles
Yellow River, 3,395 miles
Heilongjiang River, 2,159 miles
Pearl River, 1,442 miles

Ethnic Groups

Han Chinese, 91.6 %
Zhuang, 1.27%
Hui (Muslim), 0.79%
Manchu, 0.78%
Uyghur (Turkish Mus-
lims), 0.76%
Miao, 0.71%
Yi, 0.65%
Tujia, 0.63%
Tibetans, 0.47%
Mongols, 0.45%

National Language

Chinese

Dialects

1. Mandarin (taught in all schools as standard Chinese; 70% of the population only speaks this dialect)

2. Wu (spoken by 7% of the population, mostly in Shanghai)

3. Yue (aka Cantonese, spoken by 6% of the population, mostly in Guangdong Province)

4. Min (aka Fukkienese, spoken by 5% of the population, mostly in Fujian Province)

5. Xiang (aka Hunanese, spoken by 3% of the population, mostly in Hunan Province)

6. Hakka (spoken by 2.5% of the population)

7. Gan (spoken by 2% of the population

Languages spoken by 1% or less of the population

Zhuang
Mongolian
Uyghur
Turkish
Tibetan

31

Differences Between Chinese and Japanese Cultures

Some people in the West who have never traveled to China or Japan tend to view the Chinese and Japanese cultures as basically the same. It is true that almost everything we think of as traditionally Japanese was actually borrowed from China. For several millennia, Chinese government, technology, and culture were far more advanced than Japan's. The ancient Chinese kingdoms were united into one large state by the Qin emperor in 221 BC, while Japan did not even become a unified state until the early part of the sixth century AD. By then China had already produced some of the world's greatest books, including the *Dao De Jing* ("Tao Te Ching") and the *Analects* or sayings of Confucius—seven or eight centuries before Japan even had a written language.

In the 4th and 5th centuries AD, Chinese missionary monks and government emissaries brought to Japan everything from Buddhism to chopsticks. Recognizing the superiority of Chinese civilization at the time, the Japanese adopted the Chinese writing system, even though it was not a good fit with their very different spoken language. The Japanese also learned and adopted traditional Chinese architecture, examples of which can still be seen in the ancient Japanese cities of Nara and Kyoto. The Chinese missionaries shared the martial arts that Chinese Buddhist monks in mountain temples had developed to protect themselves from bandits. Rice cultivation, silk production, and porcelain making all eventually came to Japan from China. Many of the foods we know in English by their Japanese names are actually Chinese in origin, from "tofu" (the Chinese word for their bean curd is actually *dòufu*) to "ramen" (derived from the Chinese word *lā miàn* or "pulled noodles").

Due to the overwhelming number of things Japan long ago borrowed from China, there are, indeed, many things that the two cultures share. But Chinese and Japanese societies have always differed in many significant ways. By the 7th century, the way to power and wealth in China was increasingly through a national examination system based on learning, and not birth or military prowess. Although it was far more likely that a young man from a wealthy, educated family would be able to afford the books and tutors to allow him to excel in the exams to become a government official, there were enough cases of boys from poor families achieving high government position through self-education to preserve the ideal that any boy could even become prime minister through study. Only the position of emperor was based on birth.

Not so in Japan, where official position from the 7th through the 12th centuries was only achievable by those born into an aristocratic family, and for those born into a samurai (warrior) family from the late 12th century until the samurai were abolished as the ruling class in the late 19th century. During those seven centuries of samurai rule, Japan was dominated by a military class. China, on the other hand, was ruled for well over a millennium by scholar-officials. China lacks the warrior ideals known as *bushidō* ("the way of the warrior") that were revived by the Japanese in the early 20th century and helped guide their military actions that led to the tragedy of World War II in the Pacific.

It is in the present day, however, that the major cultural differences between the Chinese and Japanese are most readily apparent. There are the superficial differences, such as the fact that the Japanese, living in an island country, love to eat sushi and sashimi. Despite the popularity among young Chinese of sushi bars in large cities like Beijing and Shanghai, older Chinese consider eating almost anything raw, except fruit, as barbaric.

In Japan, for festivals, weddings, graduation ceremonies, and other special events, it is not unusual to see celebrants—especially women, as well as some men—dressed in traditional kimono. At some festivals in Japan large numbers of men dress as samurai to commemorate periods in their ancient history. In mainland China, in contrast, you're unlikely to see any Chinese dressed in traditional costumes anywhere but on the theater stage or in a handful of tourist parks that recreate China's past.

The languages the two cultures speak are from very different language families and reflect significant cultural differences. The Chinese spoken today tends to be very direct and does not vary much according to the person with whom one is speaking. The Japanese language maintains different levels and forms of speech, from shortened, informal speech used with friends and family members to very effusive special forms of respectful speech used to address someone superior in age and social status to the speaker.

Such differences in speaking also reflect very different cultural personalities. The Chinese people as a whole tend to be more open, talkative, and prone to joking than the Japanese, who tend to be more reserved and quiet. As a result, the Chinese have been called "the Italians of East Asia," while the Japanese have been compared to northern Europeans in their reticence. The great 20th-century writer from China, Lin YuTang, who became a best-selling author for his books written in English after emigrating to the U.S. in 1935, claimed that there was a natural chemistry between the Chinese people and Americans. Both were more likely to be outgoing, informal, and humorous, compared to cultures like those of Japan and Germany, whose strengths lay more in the areas of diligence and discipline.

The Japanese today continue to appear to Americans as much more polite and formal than the Chinese. Japanese people have an entire set of rules for the etiquette of bowing and are constantly bowing to others to show humility and respect. Bowing has not been a part of Chinese culture for many decades now. While the Japanese obey the queue even more than people in the Western world, foreigners often complain of how the Chinese people will cut in line when boarding a train or bus or when waiting at a ticket window. The Japanese have arguably the most refined code of manners and the most gracious way of speaking of any society in the world today. The Chinese, for better and worse, tend to be much less bound by etiquette and formality, in which regard they resemble many of us Americans.

One of the biggest differences between the cultures of China and Japan today has to do with the position of women. Executives of Western companies who do business in both China and Japan are generally struck by how in Japanese meetings the one woman present is usually there only to pour tea, while in Chinese meetings there is usually at least one woman present who commands the respect of both her colleagues and her Western counterparts and is often the person in charge. Before World War II, neither Chinese nor Japanese women had many rights and little or no education, but it is Chinese women who have seen the greatest progress in achieving equality with men. While men still largely hold the highest positions in government and business in both China and Japan, in Chinese cities there are many women in mid-level management and government jobs who are well accepted by their male colleagues. More Chinese women attend four-year colleges than men, while a large percentage of Japanese women attend only two-year colleges. At least half the doctors in China are women, and it has become fairly common for urban Chinese women to make more money than their husbands, which is rarely true in Japan.

There are many admirable traits shared by the Chinese and Japanese, as well as other East Asian countries, to be sure. Both Chinese and Japanese societies, influenced by Confucian thought, stress group harmony over the interests of the individual. Perhaps as a result of that ideal, both cultures emphasize humility. Neither Chinese nor Japanese people will ever accept a compliment by saying "thank you," but will always demur with a phrase such as "you're too kind" or "nothing of the sort." In both cultures, it is considered rude to speak about oneself too much or boast of one's achievements or those of a family member. And Chinese and Japanese people place a greater value on deep friendships and the sacrifices expected of true friends, as much as or more than almost any other cultures in the world.

China Today

32

●●●●●●●●●●●●●●●●●●●●●●●●●●●●●●●●●

The Communist Party

The Chinese Communist Party was founded in July 1921. Led mainly by the revolutionaries Chen Duxiu and Li Dazhao, it began with only fifty-seven members, most of whom were young men from the upper-middle and middle classes, including twenty-seven students, eleven journalists, and nine teachers. By 1949 it had gathered so much support among the Chinese people that it was able to drive the Nationalist Kuomintang government from the mainland and establish itself as the ruling power in China, as it has remained to the present day.

China has been a one-party state since 1949, with the Communist Party exercising complete power over the government. The Party structure consists of a National Party Congress with approximately two thousand delegates that meets every five years to elect a Central Committee of around two hundred members. The Central Committee then elects a "Politburo" (Political Bureau) of between twenty and twenty-five members. The Politburo constitutes the true ruling leadership of the Party and is believed to meet on a monthly basis. The Politburo designates a Standing Committee of from six to nine of its most powerful members that meets weekly and functions as the true executive authority for the Party and the nation.

The paramount leader of the Party is elected by the Central Standing Committee and simultaneously holds the offices of General Secretary, overseeing civilian Party affairs;

Chairman of the Central Military Commission, in charge of military affairs; and President, the ceremonial head of state. The current leader is Xi Jinping, who was elected at the 18th National Congress held in October 2012. After the death of Chairman Mao in 1976, the unwritten rule was that the top leadership position could not be held for more than two terms of five years each. However, in March of 2018 the two-term limit was eliminated, in effect allowing Xi Jinping to potentially become the only head of state since Mao to remain in power for life.

For administrative purposes, China is divided into thirty-three provincial-level units. These include twenty-two provinces, four municipalities (Beijing, Shanghai, Tianjin, and Chongqing), five autonomous regions (Inner Mongolia, Tibet, Xinjiang, Guangxi, and Ningxia), and two Special Administrative Regions (Hong Kong and Macau).

Every province (except Hong Kong and Macau, the two special administrative regions) has a provincial committee, headed by a secretary. The Committee Secretary is effectively in charge of the province, rather than the nominal governor of the provincial government.

A municipality is a higher level of city and is directly under the Chinese central government, with status equal to that of the provinces. In practice, a city's political status is higher than that of a province.

An autonomous region is a large area of land with a large population of a particular minority ethnic group. Like provinces, an autonomous region has its own local government but theoretically is given more legislative authority. The governor of each autonomous region is usually appointed from its respective minority ethnic group.

The governors of China's provinces and autonomous regions and mayors of its centrally controlled municipalities are appointed by the central government in Beijing after receiving the nominal consent of the National People's Congress. The two special administrative regions of Hong Kong and Macau have some local autonomy since they have separate governments, legal systems, and basic constitutional laws, but they come under Beijing's control in matters of foreign policy and national security, and their chief executives are handpicked by the central government.

The Chinese Communist Party has a hierarchy of Party organizations in every city, town, village, and neighborhood across the country, as well as in major workplaces and even in universities. Regulations require that all state-owned enterprises and private companies operate Party branches as well, and even some foreign-owned companies like Walmart have them.

It may surprise most Americans to learn that, in a nation of over 1.4 billion people, the Communist Party currently has only around 89 million members. That means only one in sixteen people in China is a member of the Party. And yet these members hold nearly every top position in the government, the military, education, state-owned enterprises, health care, and banking. Without membership in the Party, it is difficult to rise to any fairly high position in most organizations in China.

The acceptance rate of applicants to the Party in recent years is on a par with that of Ivy League schools in the U.S. For example, in 2014 approximately two million applicants were accepted from a pool of twenty-two million. An applicant's family background, gender, rural or urban roots, academic performance, university ranking, and perceived loyalty are all considered when determining who is accepted into the Party.

Party members are overwhelmingly male (75%), have at least a junior college education (43%), and are made up of farmers (30%), white-collar workers (25%), retirees (18%), and government employees (8%). Universities have become the main place to recruit new members, with students now constituting around 40% of those chosen for Party membership.

Leaders believe that the Party has become too large and unwieldy, so in recent years the number of new members has decreased. To be accepted into the Party, even after a candidate has been given preliminary approval, he or she has to pass a two-hour examination about Marxism, Mao Zedong thought, Deng Xiaoping theory, and other ideologies and histories that the Party considers essential. After that, the candidate is interviewed concerning their family background and career aspirations.

Party members generally will list their membership on resumés. State-owned enterprises ask about Party membership on job applications. Even in the private sector, entrepreneurs prefer to hire Party members. Party membership is viewed as a valuable credential, because it shows that the individual has been vetted by the Party and found reliable. The connections that membership brings are also invaluable to the individual and to the organization for which they work.

Given that China is ruled by an authoritarian government and headed by a political party that only includes a little more than 6% of the population, citizens of democratic countries like the U.S. likely imagine that the people of China are extremely dissatisfied with their political system. However, the large majority of Chinese people actually feel more positive about their government than Americans do about theirs.

That is likely because the standard of living for most Chinese has risen steadily and markedly over the past four decades. The tacit agreement between the government and the Chinese people has seemed to be that as long as the government continues to improve the lives of its citizens economically, it will be supported by the people. There are tens of thousands of protests each year in China, but these mostly aim to seek financial compensation or to fight environmental pollution rather than to demand substantive rights, and they often involve fewer than a couple dozen people.

Should China's economic growth begin to slow in a sizable way, resulting in tens of millions of unemployed people, the government's legitimacy will begin to be questioned. However, for the time being the people of China seem to choose social stability over political freedom, in a country that has never experienced democracy but continues to enjoy a rising standard of living for the majority of its people.

33

• •

The Chinese Military

Americans in recent years have heard from both the administration in Washington and from the Pentagon about the increasing military threat the U.S. faces from China. What they do not hear is how overwhelmingly superior the U.S. military is to that of the Chinese, even with China's growing military strength.

According to ArmedForces.eu, a reporting organization that assembles data from a multitude of sources including U.S. government reports and the C.I.A., the United States has 7,200 nuclear warheads, whereas China has but 260. The U.S. has a far bigger navy than China, with 500 warships compared to China's 300. While the U.S. boasts 20 aircraft carriers, China has but 2. The U.S. navy maintains 85 destroyers to China's 32.

The U.S. also has far superior air power. China has the world's second-largest fleet of jet fighters with 1,500, but the U.S. Air Force far surpasses that number with 2,800. Despite reports that China may overtake the U.S. in air superiority by 2030, Air Force Gen. Lori J. Robinson has emphasized that training and support for U.S. pilots gives them an "unbelievably huge" advantage over Chinese pilots.

Its vastly superior military power notwithstanding, the U.S. continues to far outspend China on its armed forces. The U.S. annual military budget currently stands at $554 billion, 3.8% of GDP. China's annual military budget is $215 billion, merely 1.9% of their GDP, which is itself only a little over half of America's GDP.

One advantage China has is its massive population, around four and a half times that of the U.S. China counts more than 2.3 million active service members, and another 1.1 million in reserves, although that has decreased from more than 3 million in active service back in the early 1990s. The U.S. has about 1.4 million active service members, with 811,000 reserves. Although the U.S. has fewer troops than China, the number of U.S. military personnel represents a much higher percentage of the population serving in the military than in China. More significantly, while the U.S. military has been engaged in war after war over the past seven decades, the last time China's military was engaged in a conflict was a short period of limited fighting with Vietnam in 1979. The Chinese have not been in a sustained conflict since the Korean War ended in 1953, and thus their troops have no experience in real battle.

By its own admission, China has deficiencies in training, cooperation between services, administration, force development, and logistics. Under the rule of the Communist Party, the Chinese military has long had to avoid honest self-assessment and focuses instead on presenting only positives to the country at large, while its forces fail to gain any experience in or practice for combat.

Furthermore, China lacks military allies to support them. In contrast, since World War II the U.S. has maintained strong alliances with its many NATO allies. Despite recently closing hundreds of military bases in Iraq and Afghanistan, the United States still maintains nearly 800 military bases in more than seventy countries and territories abroad. Britain, France and Russia have about 30 foreign bases combined. And China has but 1 overseas military base, which opened just a few years ago in the small African country of Djibouti.

Nevertheless, the U.S. continues to see China as a military threat. The Congressional Research Service, in a report to Congress in 2016, stressed that in recent years China's military has increasingly focused on strengthening its position outside its immediate periphery, "a modernization effort that could one day pose greater risks to U.S. interests in Asia and beyond." A recent report from the RAND Corporation, a California-based think tank that does research and analysis on behalf of the U.S. military, states that "the range and capabilities of Chinese air and sea defenses have continued to grow, making U.S. forward-basing more vulnerable and the direct defense of U.S. interests in the region potentially more costly.... Neither the United States nor China is likely to employ nuclear weapons, but even an initially localized conflict could quickly spread into the economic, cyber, and space realms, doing considerable damage to both sides."

China's military up to this point has almost exclusively concentrated on protecting its borders and the territorial waters surrounding China. Nevertheless, the U.S. government is concerned that China is on course to deploy greater quantities of missiles with greater ranges than defensive systems that could be employed by the U.S. Navy against them. The Department of Defense has reported that the Chinese Air Force is "rapidly closing the gap with Western air forces across a broad spectrum of capabilities" and that China "might endeavor to shift its focus from territorial air defense to both defense and offense."

There are already "soft" confrontations between the military superpowers. It is undeniable that the Chinese will increasingly seek to confront countries it sees as its enemies with media and propaganda, legal actions, and psychological warfare. China has already employed its media apparatus against the U.S. in denouncing freedom-to-navigation exercises in the South China Sea. The Chinese navy and air force have also warned off some American ships or planes that have ventured close to islands in the South China Sea that China has been recently developing. There have been numerous and credible reports that China has used cyber espionage to steal U.S. military secrets.

Whether or not China should be seen as a serious military threat to the U.S. depends largely on whether or not you hold the belief that the U.S. should continue to try to exercise military control over the Asia-Pacific region in the future.

34

China's Population

You probably know that China has the largest population of any country in the world. What you might not know is that the population of China is a smaller percentage of the world's total population today than at almost any time in the past two to three thousand years.

For most of human history China had on average one-quarter of the world's people. Two thousand years ago, at the time of Christ and at the height of the Roman Empire, China had approximately 50 million people, while there were around 45 million people living under Roman rule. Together the two empires comprised nearly half of the world's population. By the year 1000, when the world population was 275 million, the Chinese population of 80 million made up between one-third and one-fourth of all people on earth. By the middle of the 19th century, when the world's population had ballooned to 1.2 billion people, the Chinese population had grown to around 300 million, almost exactly one-fourth of that total. The U.N. puts the current Chinese population at a little over 1.413 billion people, or 18.54% of world population.

The reason for this proportionate decrease in Chinese people is that China's family planning practices over the past thirty to forty years have produced a decline in China's growth rate. It now is 159th in the world at just a little over 1.1 children on average born to women of childbearing age.

The Chinese government began in the 1960s to try to limit family size by encouraging late marriage and by promoting the ideal family as consisting of two children for city residents and three to four children for those in rural areas. By the early 1970s China had enacted an aggressive family-planning policy, and its fertility rate began to drop rather significantly. As is well known in the West, in 1979 the government began to heavily promote a far more drastic policy of mandating a one-child limit per couple in both urban and rural areas, although rural families whose first child was a girl or disabled were allowed to have a second child. By the mid-1980s the 8–9% of the population who belonged to one of the fifty-five minorities who were not Han-Chinese were allowed at least two children per couple, and there was no limit for any ethnic group that was particularly small in number. The population of China in 1979 when the stringent family-planning measures first went into effect was around 981 million. The hope was to limit China's population to only 1.2 billion by the year 2000, in order to raise the standard of living of what was then one of the poorer countries in the world.

What happened instead was that the Chinese population increased to 1.263 billion by 2000, growing by nearly the size of the population of the U.S. at the time in only twenty years. Urban residents did become convinced of the desirability of having only one child, since they were given benefits such as cash bonuses, better child care, and preferential housing and because raising a child in a city was very expensive. What the family-planning officials did not figure on was that the 60% of Chinese who were still living in rural areas in the last few decades of the 20th century would not be as willing to cooperate with the program, and instead wanted to ensure they would have enough sons to help with the farming and to take care of them in old age.

Nevertheless, there has been a dramatic decline in fertility in China in the first two decades of the 21st century, from 1.55 children per woman of childbearing age to a little over 1.1. In great part this has been due to the huge migration to the cities from the countryside during this time, which has reduced the rural population from 60% of the whole to less than 42%. This in turn has created a housing shortage in the cities, coinciding with a huge increase in the expense of raising and educating a child there.

The Chinese government officially ended the "one-child policy" on January 1, 2016 and now allows all couples to have two children. The government's concern was that the population was aging too quickly, which would result in too few people of working age to support the rapidly growing number

of retired people and sustain an expanding economy. Already over 11% of the population is sixty-five years of age or older (158 million), with 17.3% of the population age sixty and above (240 million). The planners were also concerned with census data in 2010 that revealed there were around 118 boys born for every 100 girls. With 9 million more boys than girls at present, the fear is that when the children grow up there will be a shortage of women for the men to marry.

But problems remain. When the "one-child policy" was eliminated, the family planners overestimated how many couples would decide to have a second child. Only a fairly small percentage of couples opted for another baby, having already tasted the benefits of providing for but a single child. An increasing number of couples are deciding to not have any children at all. And given the employment opportunities now open to women, a number of Chinese women for the first time in history are choosing to remain single.

Still, despite the very low birth rate in China, the

population is increasing, albeit at a much slower pace than previously. This is due both to the great reduction in infant mortality and to the vastly increased life expectancy over just the past four decades. Life expectancy at birth has now reached 76.4 years. That's an increase of nearly ten years from the figure of 66.5 years in 1980, shortly after the "one-child policy" was put into effect. In the largest cities in China life expectancy now is almost on a par with that in developed countries like the U.S.

Projections are that the population of China will reach its peak of 1.44 billion in 2030, when it will only account for around 16.5% of the projected world population of 8.6 billion. It is then projected to decline to 1.36 billion by 2050, a reduction to 14% of the projected world population of 9.8 billion. By 2100, when the projected population of the world is 11.2 billion, it is estimated that China's population will be only 1.02 billion, an amount equal to 9% of the world's population. By that time India is projected to have 500 million more people than China, with Nigeria being the third most populous nation with 800 million and the U.S. at number four with 450 million.

35

● ●

China's Biggest Cities

Since China is the most populous nation on earth, most people assume it has the biggest cities in the world. But the most populous urban areas in the world are not in China.

However, the number of cities in the People's Republic with very large populations may surprise you, even considering that China has 18% of the world's population.

Statistics for the population of a city depend on how "city" is defined. Figures can be given for the "city proper," which is based on the administrative boundary. Other figures take into consideration "urban concentration," which includes the urban or built-up areas that adjoin the city's boundaries. A third definition of "city" is the greater metropolitan area, which includes any outlying areas that are interconnected with the city proper economically and socially.

Based on this third definition, there are thirty-one "megacities" or huge metropolitan areas in the world. China contains six of these, the most of any country, while India has five. The largest megacity is the greater Tokyo area, with around 38 million people, between one-third and one-fourth of the entire population of Japan. Delhi, India, is second with around 26.5 million people.

Shanghai is the largest Chinese city in population and #3 in the world, with approximately 24.5 million. As might be expected, Beijing is the second most populous city in China, with more than 21 million, and the sixth largest metropolitan area in the world. The other largest cities in China include Chongqing in Sichuan Province in the southwest, with close to 14 million, #16 in the world; Guangzhou (known in English as Canton) in Guangdong Province in the southeast with nearly 13 million, #19; Tianjin in the northeast with around 11.5 million, #24; and Shenzhen, Guangdong Province, with nearly 11 million people, #26. By comparison, the U.S. has only one megacity, New York, which has approximately 18.6 million people, making it the 10th largest metropolitan area in the world, although the population of the city proper is only 9 million (the figure most Americans know).

China's urban population has grown enormously since the

early 1980s when people in the countryside and smaller cities and towns were free to migrate to the large cities. The most stunning example of the rapid urbanization of China since the economic and social reforms began around four decades ago is Shenzhen. Whereas Beijing had been the capital of China for centuries, and cities like Shanghai and Guangzhou were long ago established as major commercial centers, as late as 1979 Shenzhen was just a cluster of small fishing villages with a total of fewer than thirty thousand inhabitants. When it was declared a "Special Economic Zone" in 1980, making it into one of a handful of test cases for capitalism in China, the town transformed within less than forty years into a metropolis of more than 11 million people. That figure doesn't even fully count the great numbers of migrant workers who stay in the city for periods of several months or more at a time.

If cities are more narrowly defined as including only the "city proper," i.e., within the administrative boundaries of the urban area, then China has 102 cities with populations over a million. The U.S. by contrast has only ten. One result of this increasing concentration of the Chinese population is the high level of air pollution in China. The U.S. per capita emits more than twice as much carbon emissions into the atmosphere as does China, but smog is so much worse in China due to the greater population density in its cities.

With the continuing flood of people into the cities from the countryside in China, for the first time in Chinese history more than half the Chinese population now live in urban areas. This trend is expected to continue for some decades to come as China continues to develop its economy.

36

Economic Growth and the Rise in Personal Income

Alarms about China raised by our politicians and the media in the past several decades led nearly half of Americans to believe that China's economy is now number one in the world, surpassing that of the U.S. According to some estimates, China's GDP in 2017, measured in U.S. dollars, was $11.9 trillion, which is only 62% that of the U.S. economy. Given that China has four and a half times the population of the U.S., this means that China's per capita GDP in 2017 of $8,583 was just a little more than 14% that of the U.S. Moreover, leading economic analysts predict that China's GDP growth will slow considerably in the years ahead and will eventually be on a par with U.S. growth rates by the year 2036.

Nevertheless, the growth in the Chinese economy from the beginning of economic reforms in 1979 through the present has been truly astounding and has resulted in a dramatic increase in the standard of living for the majority of Chinese people. Before the economic reforms and liberalization of trade nearly forty years ago, the Chinese government maintained policies that kept the economy extremely backward, stagnant, centrally controlled, vastly inefficient, and relatively isolated from the global economy.

Since opening up to foreign trade and investment and implementing free-market reforms in 1979, China has been among the world's fastest-growing economies. Real annual gross domestic product (GDP) growth has averaged 9.5% through 2017, a pace described by the World Bank as "the fastest sustained expansion by a major economy in history." This has allowed China to double its GDP every eight years and helped raise an estimated eight hundred million people out of poverty. China is now the world's greatest manufacturer and trader of goods, as well as the largest holder of foreign exchange reserves.

The result of this phenomenal economic growth has been a dramatic increase in the annual income of the average Chinese citizen. In 1978, just before the liberalization of the economy, the median per capita income was only 343 RMB (Chinese dollars), or around $34 U.S. dollars at the exchange rate of the time. It's true that the government provided free housing in tiny apartments for city residents, as well as free education, and that food was extraordinarily cheap, albeit rationed. But the Chinese people were extremely poor and had little or no access to Western goods, and would not have been able to afford them even had they been available. By 1985 the average per capita income had more than doubled to 711 RMB, approximately 70 U.S. dollars. Nevertheless the Chinese people as a whole remained very poor.

China's "economic miracle" allowed the personal annual income of the average Chinese citizen to rise to 15,780 RMB by 2008. And in 2018 it reached close to 36,400 RMB, which at the exchange rate at the time was about $5,800 per year. That is nearly 160 times the annual income in 1979.

As impressive as that increase may be, China's median per capita income is only 55% of the world average per capita income of $12,981. By contrast, the median per capita income in the U.S. in 2016 was $46,550, six to seven times higher than that of the Chinese. China has created a middle class of around 150 million people who can afford to buy goods from the U.S. and other developed nations. But the great majority of Chinese are still far poorer than the great majority of Americans, despite any misconceptions some Americans may harbor.

37

Gender Equality

Up until the 20th century women in China were among the most oppressed of any women in the world. According to the Confucian dictum followed by Chinese society for well over two thousand years, women's lot was to yield to men. As girls they were taught to obey their fathers, after marriage be subservient to their husbands, and after their husband's death be governed by their sons. Except for some notable women among the wealthy, educated class, women were not schooled at all. Confucius taught that if women were to remain virtuous, they should not receive an education.

Girls in a family were seen as a financial burden, since as soon as they reached puberty they would be married off to someone in another village or town and not serve their own family in any way as an adult. Many families sold their young daughters to other families as servants, and when the girl reached maturity she would be married to a man in that family who often was decades older than her.

Women could either be wives, concubines, or prostitutes.

Most women were married off by their families as soon as they reached puberty, and sometimes even before that. All marriages were arranged by the parents of the couple involved and were simply an economic arrangement between the families. Husbands could divorce their wives at any time for almost any reason and with impunity, while wives had no right to divorce their husbands. Women who were sold by their families to be a concubine had even less freedom in their actions than did wives; they were kept as formal mistresses by men for sexual services and to produce children. Women who became prostitutes were frequently women sold into brothels by their parents if the family was too poor to be able to afford to raise them.

It wasn't until the late 19th and early 20th centuries that a growing number of women began to receive an education in schools run by Western missionaries. Even though they were a small minority among all Chinese women, many of them took part in the revolution that brought the Communist Party to power in 1949. In dramatic and sweeping fashion, the Communist Party freed women from all of the oppressive restraints of traditional Confucian society. The buying and selling of girls and women was outlawed. So, too, were polygamy and arranged marriages. For the first time in Chinese history, it was possible for couples to marry for love. The custom of foot-binding, which had crippled approximately half of all Chinese women by the early 20th century, was strongly condemned. And for the first time all girls as well as all boys were to receive an education, rather than just the sons of the wealthy.

The Constitution of the People's Republic of China, enacted in 1954, explicitly stated that women and men should have equal rights. To promote gender equality, the Communist Party preached the slogan "women hold up half the sky" to emphasize the importance of women to China's growing economic success.

In order to further equality of the sexes, the Chinese government implemented policies that guaranteed equal pay for equal work, as well as equal job opportunities for women and men. In practice, however, gender inequality in pay still existed in the workplace under the socialist planned economy China maintained until 1979. This is because women tended to be in the lower-paid occupations and industries. After China's market-oriented reforms were more fully realized in the 1990s and early 2000s, gender inequality in Chinese labor markets has actually become even worse and is now recognized as a major economic and social problem. In the past three decades migrant women coming into the large cities from the countryside for work have been used as a cheap source of labor. They make up the great majority of factory workers, shop clerks, and waitresses, as well as serving as maids and domestic workers for wealthier Chinese. These roles make these women particularly vulnerable to exploitation due to the lack of public scrutiny of their workplaces. They have, however, been vital to the success of China's free market economy. Without their low-cost labor, China would not have been so successful in competing with other countries in manufacturing. A 2013 study found that overall women were paid 75.4% of what men were paid.

By international standards, gender equality in China is considered relatively low, especially when compared to the high ideals claimed by the Communist government. In 2014 China ranked as the 40th least equal society in the United Nations Development Program's Gender Inequality Index. This index measures gender inequalities in 187 nations in three important aspects of human development: reproductive health as measured by maternal mortality ratio and adolescent birth rates; empowerment, as measured by the percentage of seats in the national legislature held by women, as well as by the proportion of women and men over the age of twenty-five with at least some secondary education; and economic status as seen in the relative proportion of women and men over age fifteeen in the labor force.

China received low marks in maternal mortality ratio, which was 32 out of 100,000 live births. Only 58.7% of women aged twenty-five or older had completed secondary or higher education, versus 71.9% of Chinese men. The percentage of women in the labor force was merely 63.9% compared to 78.3% for men. And women accounted for only 23.6% of representatives in the national assembly. Actually, in these last two categories, China actually scores higher than the U.S., where only 57% of women hold jobs, and—until the November 2018 midterm elections—merely 19% of the members of the U.S. House of Representatives and 23% of the members of the U.S. Senate were women.

Of course the position of women in Chinese society is far better than it was before the Communist government came to power. Women are no longer subject to foot-binding or arranged marriages. They are given the opportunity for equal education with men and have the same legal rights. Approximately half of all doctors in China are women, and there are a number of Chinese women who hold executive positions in major companies. Women in the largest cities are arguably as equal with men as women in the U.S. are. However, without strict government regulations that protect women's rights, in part due to a high level of corruption and hypocrisy, gender inequality will continue to be a major problem in China today, most especially for less-educated women from the countryside and for those from less-developed smaller cities.

38

Marriage and Divorce

Since the economic and social reforms that began in the late 1970s, Chinese society has experienced many dramatic changes. In merely forty years China has gone from one of the poorest and most isolated countries to the number two economy in the world. As many as eight hundred million people have been lifted out of poverty as the world's largest migration of people occurred in just a little over a generation. Nearly two hundred million people have moved from the countryside into the cities, increasing the percentage of the population in urban areas from 18% of the total to more than 58% today.

It is hardly surprising that such cataclysmic changes would be accompanied by equally dramatic social changes. One aspect of Chinese life that has witnessed a sea change is marriage and divorce. Until the 1980s, the vast majority of the adult population got married and divorce was extremely rare. As recently as 1986 only around 5% of adults were single and the divorce rate stood at just 0.9%. Currently close to 15% of adults are single, while the divorce rate has skyrocketed to 4.5%. Over 40% of divorces occur within the first five years of marriage, with the average age of a first marriage being twenty-six, compared to twenty-seven for women in the U.S. and twenty-nine for men.

While the divorce rate in China is half that in Japan and a fraction of that in the U.S., what is troubling to many in China is how rapid the increase has been. And China's divorce rate is climbing faster than the rate of new marriages. The shift is even more pronounced in major cities like Shanghai, where divorces were up 13% and marriages actually decreased by 3% in 2017. And although the percentage of marriages ending in divorce for the country as a whole seems fairly insignificant in comparison to Western nations, in Beijing currently 39% of marriages now end in divorce, almost on a level with the U.S.

Many reasons are given for the rising divorce rate. Most relationship experts and lawyers in China attribute it to higher expectations concerning marriage and the growing financial independence among women. For the first time in Chinese history, more than half the people live in urban areas, where they have much greater freedom than they had when living with their parents in rural villages. Many women in the cities have an income equal to or greater than that of their husbands and can afford to support themselves if a marriage turns sour. And unlike older generations who may have settled for an unhappy marriage, divorce is no longer socially taboo in China.

China also makes it rather easy to obtain a divorce. Couples can register a divorce with the civil affairs authority, indicating they have agreed to go their separate ways, or they can sue for divorce through the courts, which can rule on custody of children and how to dispose of any assets. A little over three decades ago, in 1986, 460,000 couples registered their divorces with the civil affairs authority, the most common route taken. By 2016 that annual number had risen to 4.15 million.

By far the leading cause of divorce in China is extramarital affairs. The China Marriage and Family Affairs Consulting and Research Center estimated that in 2011 70% of divorces were a result of infidelity. Chinese marriage experts and divorce lawyers blame the influence of Western culture for the increasing number of young people in China pursuing romantic relationships. Social networks also make finding a one-night stand much easier, they point out.

The second leading cause of divorce is domestic violence. Courts in Beijing report that in the past year 93% of its divorce cases involved either spousal abuse or extramarital affairs. A legal aid center for women in Beijing blames a social environment that has been highly tolerant of domestic violence. In a survey done by Jiayuan, a dating website, 18% of female divorcees said they filed for divorce because they were physically abused by their husbands, and 38% wanted a divorce because their husband cheated on them, while 25% of men who sought a divorce cited infidelity by their wives as the reason.

While the divorce rate has soared in recent years, compared to a generation ago, there are reasons for the drop in the rate of new marriages as well. For one thing, China's population control policies, along with some Chinese families' traditional preference to have sons rather than daughters, have created a serious demographic imbalance. There are now thirty-four million more young men than women.

One consequence of this is that the groom's family must pay higher and higher prices for the betrothal gifts that have been part of Chinese weddings since ancient times. In just the past four years, according to a study conducted by the state-run *People's Daily* newspaper, the cost of betrothal gifts in Beijing has risen more than twentyfold.

An average groom in Beijing now has to present his prospective in-laws with a 200,000 yuan ($30,000) cash gift and buy an apartment for his future wife to win their daughter's hand in marriage.

Famous Figures in Chinese History

 Confucius (551–479 B.C.), a philosopher and teacher whose teachings became the governing philosophy of Chinese rulers for several millennia

 Qin Shi Huang (259–210 B.C.), founder of the Qin dynasty and the first emperor of a unified China

Wu Zetian (Empress Wu; 624–705), the only woman to ever rule China as emperor

 An Lushan (703–757), a general in the Tang dynasty whose bloody rebellion nearly toppled the emperor

 Zheng He (1371–1433), a Chinese mariner, explorer, and fleet admiral whose seven expeditionary voyages to southern and western Asia as well as East Africa from 1405 to 1433 may have given rise to the legend of Sinbad the Sailor

 Hong Xiuquan (1814–64), leader of the Taiping Rebellion who established his own kingdom in parts of southern China, declaring himself the "Heavenly King" and self-proclaimed younger brother of Jesus Christ

 Yung Wing (1828–1912), the first Chinese student to graduate from an American university who brought 120 students from China to study in the U.S. on the Chinese Educational Mission from 1872 to 1881

39

• •

The LGBTQ Community

Ancient China had a long history of tolerance toward homosexuality. Same-sex love and intercourse were quite common and accepted among males for centuries, especially within the royal family and among the scholarly class. Since women weren't educated, intellectuals in particular enjoyed their closest bonds with other men. As long as they fulfilled their duty of carrying on the family line by marrying and having children, men were free to engage in these relationships.

It was not until the May Fourth Movement (1917–21) and the opening up to Western ideas that the concept of "homosexuality" as sexual perversion was introduced into China. After the establishment of the People's Republic of China in 1949, homosexuality became taboo and was rarely discussed.

In the 1980s homosexuality was only mentioned in China in studies on sex and psychology as a perversion and abnormality, a product of Western capitalism. Although there was no specific law against homosexual behavior, homosexuals could be arrested and punished under the crime of hooliganism. Nevertheless, in China there was never the bitter condemnation of homosexuality seen in the U.S. because the Chinese lacked any religious conviction that such sexual orientation was a sin.

One of the many dramatic social changes in China can be seen in how attitudes toward homosexuality have evolved in just the past few decades. In 1997 adult consensual and non-commercial homosexuality was declared legal. It took until 2001, however, for homosexuality to be removed from the Ministry of Health's official list of mental illnesses. The public health campaign to fight the HIV/AIDS pandemic amazingly now includes education for men who have sex with other men. Officially, overt police actions against gay people is restricted to sex acts in public and prostitution, which are also illegal for heterosexuals.

Until the 21st century, almost all gays and lesbians were careful to hide their sexual orientation. However, in a survey of 18,650 lesbians, gay, bisexual, and transgender people conducted recently by an organization that aims to support the LGBTQ community in China, 3% of the males and 6% of the females surveyed described themselves as "completely out." A third of the men as well as 9% of the women surveyed said they were in the closet about their sexuality. Some 18% of men surveyed answered they had come out to their families, while around 80% were reluctant to do so due to family pressure. That at least some LGBTQ people in China now feel free to be open about their sexuality is one of a great many ways that Chinese society has made strides toward more personal freedom in areas that are not perceived by the government to threaten their authority.

In April 2018, the popular microblogging site Sina Weibo, China's equivalent of Twitter, announced a new policy to ban all pieces of content related to pornography, violence, and homosexuality. According to the site, they were following a directive by the "Network Cyber Security Law." However, the newest version of that law, which the government put into effect in June 2017, only stated that media involving pornography was banned. The issue of homosexuality was not mentioned. It remains unclear if Sina Weibo's decision reflected the company's own prejudicial attitude or if it hinted at some future government policy against the LGBTQ community.

In any case, given the power of the Web in today's China

and the increasing self-confidence among the LGBTQ community, a great many people both inside and outside that community expressed real anger at Weibo's announcement. The same day that Weibo declared its new policy, a Weibo user named Zhu Dingzhen simply posted, "I am gay. What about you?" The post was read more than 2.4 billion times and shared by nearly 3 million users, commented on by 1.5 million users, and liked by 9.5 million users in less than three days. Weibo immediately posted that it was reversing its previous decision, stating that the service would stop banning content related to homosexuality and expressed thanks to its users for their "discussions" and "suggestions."

Despite the significant strides made in LGBTQ rights in China, no civil rights law exists to address discrimination or harassment on the basis of sexual orientation or gender identity. Households headed by same-sex couples are not permitted to adopt children and do not have the same privileges as heterosexual married couples. Nevertheless, just as in the U.S., younger people are more likely to find homosexuality acceptable. According to a 2013 Pew Research Center global-wide survey on attitudes toward homosexuality, 32% of Chinese under the age of thirty think homosexuality is acceptable, compared with only 15% of those fifty and older. And in the very largest cities there seems to be real support for same-sex marriage. Research conducted in 2014 by the *Chinese Journal of Human Sexuality* showed that nearly 85% of the 921 respondents supported same-sex marriage, while a mere 2% opposed the idea, and 13% of them were "unsure."

Peng Yanhui is the founder of an LGBTQ rights advocacy group in the huge southern city of Guangzhou. Some years ago he went undercover to gather evidence that doctors were falsely advertising on the Internet a "cure" for homosexuality. Those doctors used electric shock "therapy" to try to change his sexual orientation from gay to straight. In 2014 he filed a lawsuit charging such health clinics with defrauding consumers, arguing that homosexuality had been removed from China's official registry of mental disorders in 2001. He won his case. His success emboldened more gays and lesbians to come out of the closet and to go so far as to advocate for themselves in open court.

Though China has no law to ban discrimination based on sexual orientation, some people have successfully filed lawsuits against unfair treatment based on existing statutes governing employment, consumer protection, and other issues. Members of the LGBTQ community are not always successful in their lawsuits, but the very fact that they now dare to defend their rights in the law courts is astounding enough. What is even more heartening is that they sometimes win. In the past few years a gay husband was awarded damages and an apology from a mental institution that colluded with his estranged wife to lock him up for treatment for nineteen days. A gay food safety technician won an appeal against an employer who suspended him after he tested HIV positive. And a judge ruled recently that a transgender man was unlawfully fired simply because he refused to dress like a woman at work.

Even when LGBTQ members lose in court, some of their cases become high-profile enough to attract domestic as well as international attention from the media. Just last year a gay couple sued unsuccessfully to obtain a marriage license. Two months later a twenty-one-year-old lesbian journalism student took the Chinese Ministry of Education to court for approving inaccurate descriptions of homosexuality in university textbooks—she lost her suit. Members of the movement for LGBTQ rights feel that the main objective at this point is not so much to win their legal cases as to increase visibility and build identity. This is the only way to beat a regime of censorship like that in China.

While Chinese society has seen a tightening of control in recent years, LGBTQ communities have flourished online and generally under the radar. They organize through Sina Weibo and hold weekly live video chats to gain followers. A Guangzhou-based organization has fifty-two chapters across the country, including some in smaller cities. Beijing's LGBTQ Center raises its profile and donations by holding monthly fundraisers at restaurants and bars. The activities celebrating International Day Against Homophobia 2018 in China were unprecedentedly large. Many college students voluntarily stood on the streets distributing rainbow badges, wristbands, and flyers to the public as a way to show their support to LGBTQ groups.

40

• •

China's Youth

The rapid economic growth of China over the last four decades has created enormous social changes in Chinese society. Inevitably these changes have affected young people in China more than any other group. Eric Fish, a journalist working at the Asia Society in New York, wrote an insightful book in 2015 entitled *China's Millennials: The Want Generation*. Fish points out that in China the older generations regard the younger generation as extremely spoiled, growing up as they have in the new and prosperous China, and incapable of understanding the hardships their parents and grandparents endured when China was poor. The stereotype regarding

China's youth held by foreigners is that they are not the idealists of the 1980s who protested in Tiananmen Square in 1989 for greater freedoms but are materialistic, nationalistic, and anti-foreign.

Based on his research while teaching English and working as a journalist in China from 2007 to 2014, Fish discovered the reality is quite different. What he learned was that the greater economic and personal freedoms that China has enjoyed since the 1980s have made young people in China, including both urban and rural youth, much more ambitious, with much loftier goals than those of the previous generation. In today's economy, a significant percentage of young Chinese no longer belong to an established work unit that in the past would completely control every aspect of a worker's life. This has given young people in China unprecedented individual freedom and a willingness to challenge authority. They are standing up for their rights far more than Chinese youth ever did in the past. For example, factory protests and strikes have seen a huge increase from a total of only 8 in 2011 to 503 in 2015.

One major change in the lives of Chinese people today compared to only a few decades ago is the advent of the Internet. Nearly 80% of China's teenagers are online and get their information from social media rather than from the Party via the government-controlled media. This has encouraged far greater individualism in what has always been a group-centered society. It has created counter-culture elements like what we have in the U.S. In today's China you can find every type of youth, from hipsters to hippies, Goths to Hells Angels. Before the advent of social media on the Internet, gays and lesbians felt isolated and were afraid to acknowledge their sexual orientation. Now they can go online and discover that there are a great many people who are like them. The stunning revival of religion since the 1980s has allowed religious beliefs to proliferate. Whereas in the U.S. it's the older generations who constitute the majority of believers, in China it is the young, a great many of whom have become Christians.

By speaking to Chinese youth between the ages of eighteen and thirty-five, Eric Fish learned that they feel they have more in common with young people in other countries like the U.S. than they do with older people in their own society. Large numbers of them travel abroad, given the new affluence and the much greater freedoms that make that possible. Hundreds of thousands of them come to the U.S. and other Western countries for high school, college, or graduate school. They have a much more global perspective than do their parents or grandparents. Young people are not more nationalistic than their elders. For example, although only 37% of Chinese over the age of thirty-five have a favorable view of the U.S., 56% of those under thirty-five view the U.S. favorably.

Activism and volunteerism by the young are increasingly common. In a survey of urban youth that Fish conducted in China only a few years ago, as many as 53% of young people put a higher priority on finding a job in which they could "give back to society" and that would provide them with a sense of enjoyment and fulfillment than one that would offer a high level of pay. Many Chinese young people began engaging in environmental protests more than a decade ago. In 2007 around ten thousand high school and university students joined in a protest against a proposed chemical factory in the southern coastal city of Xiamen. There are young activists for women's causes such as combating sexual harassment and supporting LGBT rights, with some willing to be attacked and jailed in order to be a force for social change.

All of this is against a backdrop of a society in which things are actually becoming more challenging for young people, despite their new affluence and freedoms. One problem is the lack of good white-collar jobs for the rapidly increasing number of college graduates entering the work force. There are over 7.5 million new college graduates annually, an increase of 0.25 million each year. At the same time, with the economy slowing, there are 15–20% fewer jobs for these graduates to fill. As a result, there is a growing sense of disillusionment among today's educated youth.

Another challenge faced by young people in China today is growing income inequality in a society that already has one of the greatest wealth disparities in the world. For those without connections, it's ever more difficult to land a good job. When surveyed, 80% of Chinese educated youth said they thought success was more dependent on family connections than ability, with only 10% feeling that knowledge and ability were the main factors in getting ahead.

Not surprisingly, it is the large number of rural youth who have the hardest time succeeding in today's China. While 23% of Chinese millennials were born in cities, nearly 60% of them now live in cities, having moved there to seek a better life than they could expect to have if they had stayed in the countryside. They have a much lower educational level than the average person their age who grew up in the cities. When they witness how much less they have than their urban counterparts, they are understandably dissatisfied.

Yet another challenge that Chinese youth must now face, especially for the great majority who are only children, is the burden of caring for their two aging parents and four aging grandparents. This places a huge pressure on young people to find lucrative work that will provide them with a sufficient income to help their families later in life. At the same time, there is a growing generation gap in terms of social attitudes. Since most Chinese millennials place a greater priority on finding a career that will bring them satisfaction over one that will just allow them to make a lot of money, there is often a conflict between parental expectations for their child's future and what the child wants for him- or herself.

In addition, today's millennials are often not anxious to rush into marriage, and an increasing number are deciding to remain single. That puts them into serious conflict with their parents, who pressure them to marry and have children in a society that traditionally assumed that everyone would do so. While in the U.S. approximately half the adult population is single, in 1990 single adults in China only comprised 6% of the population. By 2015 that figure had risen to close to 15%, marking a huge change in Chinese society.

Finally there is the challenge for China's millennials to find a suitable mate. China has the world's greatest disparity tween the numbers of men and women, with as many as 120 boys born for every 100 girls. There are currently 20 million fewer young women of marriageable age than men.

On top of that, many urban women have sufficient incomes to allow them to remain single if they enjoy the freedom it provides them. And educated urban women are not interested in marrying any of the huge number of men from the countryside who have taken blue-collar jobs in the cities. This huge gender imbalance has led to an increase in crime, although the overall crime rate is far lower in China than in the U.S. Studies have shown that for every 1% increase in gender imbalance in a society, there is a 4% increase in crime, particularly crimes of a sexual nature.

While life for China's youth is overall far better than that experienced by those who grew up during the Cultural Revolution in the 1960s and 1970s, or even those who were teenagers during the very beginning of China's economic and social reforms in the 1980s, China's young people still face many challenges. Chinese millennials are much more complex than the stereotyped portraits of them that are prevalent both inside and outside of China.

41

● ●

Gaokao: The College Entrance Exam

Think the SATs and ACTs are stressful? The exams to get into universities in China are a whole lot tougher. These annual tests that high school students must take to enter university are known as the Gaokao (*gāo kǎo* in pinyin, pronounced "gow kow"; literally, "high exam," "short for "Higher Education Exam," 高考).

The exams last nine hours over a period of two days.

Chinese and mathematics are always two of the subjects tested. An English test was formerly required of all students, but now Japanese, Russian, or French may be taken instead. In addition, students in most parts of China must choose between two sets of subjects, either in the area of social sciences or the natural sciences. Students who choose social sciences are tested in history, politics, and geography; those who choose the natural sciences are tested in physics, chemistry, and biology.

In 2018 a record ten million young people applied to enter universities in China. Most had to take the Gaokao. A few who were considered to have outstanding or special talents did not have to take a test to be admitted to a top university.

The national college entrance exam takes place from June 7 to 9 every year. Unlike in the U.S., where high school students generally take the SATs and ACTs in their junior or senior year, Chinese students take the test at the end of their first year of high school, the equivalent of sophomore year in

American high schools, when students are mostly fifteen or sixteen years old. By then they'll have taken classes to prepare for the particular subjects they've chosen to be tested on—social sciences or natural sciences. During their last two years of high school they no longer take classes in the three subjects that they won't be studying in college. By deciding at such an early age which parts of the college entrance exam they're going to take, they've in effect made a general decision as to what their major in college and future career will probably be.

A university usually sets a fixed admission quota for each province, with a higher number of students coming from the province in which it's located. Because certain provinces have more universities and generally better ones than other provinces, students are in a sense discriminated against based on the area of China they live in. For example, Beijing has a great many more universities and of far better quality than Jiangxi Province in the southeast. As a result, many fewer students from Jiangxi get accepted into university compared to students from Beijing. A student from Jiangxi has to get a much higher test score than one from Beijing in order to get into the same university. Beijing University, China's very top university, in 2017 admitted 1,800 science students out of 80,000 applications from Beijing, but only 38 students from Shandong Province, even though 660,000 students from that province applied.

Because the Gaokao is such an important factor in determining a young person's future and can be taken only once a year, students are under tremendous pressure in preparing for and taking the exam. There is great pressure on the teachers, too, because they are judged on how many of their students are successful in the exams. This encourages the teachers to have their students cram for the tests by memorizing large amounts of information and by practicing writing exams. There is almost no time to teach critical thinking or to allow students to explore their values, feelings, and personalities.

Many students experience severe stress while preparing for the college entrance exam and especially while taking the test. Some are so stressed out that they faint during the exam. Many critics of this Gaokao system accuse it of being the most pressure-packed examination in the world. Despite the system's many shortcomings, it must be said that the students who do test into the top universities in China have worked a great deal harder in high school than the average American student and are far more advanced in math and science than U.S. high school graduates.

42

Favorite Music for Young People

During the first thirty years or so of Communist rule, from the 1950s through the 1970s, China didn't have much contact with the outside world. Young people in China weren't able to hear American and British pop and rock music. When China began to open up to the West in the 1980s and restrictions on Western books, films, and music were gradually lifted, younger Chinese people got to be big fans of American and British popular music.

The British rock duo Wham!, which was really big in the 1980s in the UK, became the first Western band to play in China when they gave concerts in Beijing and the southern city of Guangzhou some thirty years ago. As recently as 2002, when Kenny G came to China to perform, it was considered big news. Now it's really common for American and British rock stars to perform for huge audiences of young people in the larger Chinese cities. Taylor Swift, Bob Dylan, Robbie Williams, Bon Jovi, Michael Bublé, and Ellie Goulding have all given concerts there in recent years.

However, China is still not as free a country as the U.S. by any means.

Before foreign artists can perform in China, the government runs background checks and has to approve in advance the songs that foreign rock groups can perform. In 2006, the Rolling Stones were told to drop five songs, including "Honky Tonk Woman" and "Let's Spend the Night Together," because they hinted about sex.

Other artists have been banned completely. Jay-Z had permission for a 2006 concert turned down because of his "vulgar lyrics." Elton John was visited by the Chinese police when he announced he was dedicating his 2012 concert in Beijing to the artist and activist Ai Weiwei; the police tried to convince him to not make his concert into a political statement.

It might surprise you that the favorite songs of Chinese young people today are pretty much the same as the most popular rock and pop songs for young people in the U.S. Lady Gaga, Justin Bieber, and Rihanna are hugely popular in China. Although most Chinese do not speak English fluently, many can still easily sing an entire English pop song. More genres like hip-hop and R&B are also becoming increasingly popular, as are stars like The Weeknd.

The average Chinese young person listens to sixteen hours of music per week, and around two-thirds of listeners use a streaming service.

There are plenty of live music shows with packed audiences of young people. Not all of the concerts are by Western artists. Chinese pop music is also extremely popular, influenced by Korean K-pop and Japanese J-pop as well as by American and British rock music.

Young people in China today are increasingly becoming very much like American young people, and music is just one of the ways that's been obvious in recent years. This is one reason that Chinese students from the bigger cities are able to come to the U.S. for high school or college and adapt quite easily to life in America.

43

Popular Films

Over the past few years the film industry in China has seen amazing growth. American films attract big audiences among Chinese young people, and American film companies keep hoping to expand their reach in China. However, only thirty-four foreign films are allowed to be shown in Chinese theaters each year. This quota ensures that films produced in China get the best release dates and the most attention.

To get around the quota system, foreign producers have started partnering with Chinese studios to make co-productions like the film *Transformers: Age of Extinction*. What makes this strategy challenging is that the co-produced film has to be something that both Chinese and American audiences will really like. And the Chinese government won't allow a foreign film to be shown if it contains anything the censors feel is unacceptable, like too much sex or a political statement.

American films like *Avatar* and *Titanic*—no sex or politics—have proved very popular in China. But just as most American audiences prefer films in English to foreign films with subtitles, Chinese audiences would rather see films in Chinese. Such films don't need subtitles and all of the jokes translate.

That American comedies don't have much chance of becoming a hit in China is unfortunate, because Chinese audiences are particularly fond of comic films. The top two money-making films of all time in China, *The Mermaid* and *Monster Hunt*, are escapist comedies. Based on daily life in China that the Chinese audience can relate to, they allow the Chinese a few hours of laughter as an escape from their everyday problems.

Big-city life in China creates a lot of tension for people in China today, including the young. That's why escapist adventure films, like comedies, are also really popular in times of great social tension. Marvel's superhero films, with their humorous and lighthearted style, sometimes do even better in China than in the U.S. *Ant-Man*, for example, was not that successful in America but was the top-selling film in China for several weeks.

Comedies and adventures are one thing, but there are many types of films that aren't allowed to be shown. These include some types of fantasy films such as those involving time travel and anything dealing with politics. China's censors have also tried to clamp down on popular websites offering American shows like *NCIS*, *The Practice*, and *The Good Wife*, but they have been met with widespread anger among the shows' Chinese viewers. In 2014, when *The Big Bang Theory* was removed from streaming sites, angry fans went online to call China "West North Korea." The term was quickly blocked on Weibo, the Chinese version of Twitter. But Chinese young people increasingly love American films and TV shows and continue to find ways to see them, including buying DVD copies.

44

● ●

Sports

Now that a majority of Chinese live in cities, and many of them have much more free time and money than people in the countryside, sports are becoming more and more popular in China. More than a third of all Chinese enjoy doing some kind of sport. Ping-pong, badminton, basketball, and soccer are among the most popular activities.

But it is running that has now become the most important sport for ordinary Chinese people. Nearly half of all Chinese who do sports for fun include running as one of their main activities. There are now over one million marathon runners in China. The marathon held in the northeastern city of Jilin in late June 2017 attracted over thirty thousand runners.

Last year there were more than a hundred marathons in China. The runners are quite a bit younger than those in Europe or the U.S., and they spend more money on their hobby. The main group of serious Chinese runners are between thirty-six and forty-five years old, followed by the twenty-five- and thirty-five-year-olds.

Badminton and ping-pong have been popular sports in China for a very long time. Over a fifth of all Chinese play badminton and ping-pong for fun. Chinese professional table tennis and badminton players continue to be the top players in the world in those sports. The best badminton player of all time, the two-time Olympic champion and five-time world champion Lin Dan, is one of the greatest sports idols in all of China and famous throughout Asia. ESPN counts him among the hundred most famous athletes in the world.

Basketball has been really popular in China for the past fifty years. It's a cheap sport that only requires a basketball and doesn't need a big playing area, unlike baseball or soccer. Nearly a fifth of all Chinese who do sports play basketball. This has led to China becoming the biggest overseas audience for the American NBA.

Soccer is also really popular, both as something to do for fun and as a spectator sport. China is planning on setting up as many as fifty thousand soccer schools by 2025 in the hope of producing a national team that can someday compete in the World Cup the way the Japanese and Koreans do. Amateur leagues are planned and countless soccer fields will be built across China.

The Chinese Super League of professional soccer is investing hundreds of millions of dollars to bring in top foreign players and coaches to improve the level of play in China. Among the most famous soccer players who have agreed to play in China are the Argentinian Carlos Tevez, the Brazilian Hulk, and Jackson Martinez. Martinez switched from Atletico Madrid to the Guangzhou team Evergrande in 2016 for around $45 million.

Winter sports are also getting to be more popular in China. The 2022 Olympic Winter Games will be hosted in Beijing. With a great number of wealthier young Chinese getting interested in learning to ski, many winter sports companies are newly interested in selling their equipment in China. There are around 650 ski resorts in China, where there were none only twenty to thirty years ago. Even though most of these resorts can hardly compare to those in the U.S. or

Europe, with three-quarters of them having slopes that are only 300 feet high, many Chinese want to give skiing a try anyway. The number of people going to the ski resorts has almost tripled in recent years, from 5.5 million in 2009 to over 15 million in 2016.

45

Automobiles

In the 1980s and 1990s, Americans and other Western-ers rather correctly pictured China as a land where everyone got around on bicycles. The ownership of private automobiles only began in the early 1980s. As recently as 2005 the Euro-pean singer Katie Melua released her hit song "Nine Million Bicycles in Beijing." At that time most Chinese did still get around town on bicycles, when they weren't taking a bus. There were not only around nine million bicycles in China's capital city, but hundreds of millions more across the country that were ridden every day.

By 2007 there were 59 million automobiles in China and even more motorbikes. The number of cars increased by 15–20 million every year, according to the Ministry of Pub-lic Security's Traffic Management Bureau. As of 2016, vehi-cle ownership had reached 279 million, with over 61% (194 million) being cars, marking a transition from motorcycles to automobiles as a major means of motor transportation. Bike lanes in major cities increasingly disappeared as automobiles dominated the roadways.

Among the 136 million small-sized cars, about 91.5% are privately owned, with the remainder belonging to government organizations or private enterprise companies. For every hundred households there are 31 private cars, while in big cities such as Beijing and Shenzhen estimates run as high as 60 or more. There are forty cities that have car ownership of more than 1 million. and in eleven cities including Beijing, Shanghai, Shenzhen, and Tianjin car ownership exceeds 2 million. In the year 2015 alone another 33.75 million new drivers hit the roads, raising the number of licensed drivers of automobiles to nearly 300 million by the time this book was published.

In 2010, China surpassed the U.S. and all other countries in vehicle sales, and it will no doubt remain number one for many decades. However, the rapid growth of automobile ownership in China has alarming implications for both the environment and for global energy resources. China is already the world's largest CO_2 emitter and the second largest oil importer. Yet its vehicle ownership rate is still a fraction of that in the US—58 vehicles per 1,000 persons in 2010 compared to 804 per 1,000 in the US. Clearly, the market for vehicles in China will grow. Most forecasts anticipate it leveling off at an ownership rate of about 200–300 vehicles per 1,000 persons in 2030 or shortly afterward.

China's fast growth in motorizing private transportation may threaten global oil supplies and further worsen climate change. Indeed, if China's vehicle ownership rate reaches 600 to 800 vehicles per 1,000 persons, equivalent to rates in Europe and the U.S. respectively, then China's total vehicle population would approach 1 billion. That's more than four times the number of vehicles in the United States today. Even at a much lower level of 300 vehicles per 1,000 persons, the worldwide impact would be huge. Chinese vehicles alone would consume 12–18% of all the oil produced today.

It should be noted that there are still 430 million bicycle owners in China. Although the fast multiplication of cars in China and the traffic jams they cause in urban areas dominate the news, the bicycle remains the biggest means of individual mobility for hundreds of millions Chinese.

46

●●●●●●●●●●●●●●●●●●●●●●●●●●●●●

Pollution

The U.S. media have focused in recent years on the serious problem of pollution in cities in China, showing photos of smog-choked cities like Beijing with the residents wearing masks to protect themselves. Among the nations of the world, China does contribute by far the most in carbon emissions from the burning of fossil fuels, accounting for nearly 30% of the global total. The U.S. is the second worst offender, emitting nearly 15% of the total for the world.

What is not generally acknowledged is that the U.S. produces a little less than half the carbon emissions of China, but its per capita emissions are around 2.5 times greater, since China has around 4.5 times the population of the U.S.

In addition, the popular perception in the United States of Chinese cities being the most polluted in the world is most definitely not true.

Air pollution is measured by the number of fine micrometers of particulate matter in the air produced by burning fossil fuels from motor vehicles, power plants, industry, and so on, called PM 2.5. People's health is affected when levels are high. The pollution in urban areas in Pakistan is nearly 3 times worse than in China's cities, with an average PM 2.5 figure of nearly 116, compared to China's 41.5. And ten of the twenty most polluted cities in the world are in India. China only has four cities that rank in the top twenty worst polluted, including the industrial cities of Xingtai (#9), Baoding (#10), Shijiazhuang (#14), and Handan (#19). All four of those cities are in the northern province of Hebei, the same province in which Beijing is located, and are a contributing factor to the relatively high level of air pollution in Beijing.

While their air quality is a huge concern, it's shocking to learn that China's urban areas rank as only the thirteenth most polluted in the world. India is the country with the ninth worst overall pollution, with an average PM 2.5 of over 60. The most polluted countries in the world include, in order, Pakistan, Qatar, Afghanistan, Bangladesh, Iran, Egypt, Mongolia, and the United Arab Emirates. Of course, current air-pollution levels still exceed China's own standards and far surpass the World Health Organization safety recommendations.

Another fact about air pollution in China that is not widely publicized in the West is the tremendous progress China has made in recent years in addressing this issue. On March 4, 2014, the Chinese premier, Li Keqiang, announced live on state television at a meeting of the National People's Congress that "We will resolutely declare war against pollution as we declared war against poverty." The Chinese government realizes they must take dramatic steps to reduce air pollution, since it caused the deaths of 1.58 million people in China in 2016, according to the Health Effects Institute.

The announced "war against pollution" signaled a dramatic change from the country's longstanding policy of emphasizing economic growth over environmental concerns. China has followed through at an astonishing pace. In the cities, concentration of fine particulates in the air from carbon

emissions has been cut by 32% on average just in the four years between 2014 and 2018.

To reach these targets, China prohibited new coal-fired power plants in the country's most polluted regions, including the Beijing area. Existing plants were told to reduce their emissions. If they failed to do so, coal was replaced with natural gas. Large cities, including Beijing, Shanghai, and Guangzhou, restricted the number of cars on the road. The country also reduced its iron- and steel-making capacity and shut down many coal mines.

After the introduction of the U.S. Clean Air Act in 1970 it took until 1982 for the country to achieve the 32% reduction in air pollution that China has achieved in just four years. China's fight against pollution will potentially allow for extraordinary gains in life expectancy. City residents across the country can be expected to live an average of nearly 2½ years longer if air pollution continues to decline at the present rate.

While China may be the planet's biggest polluter, it far surpasses all other countries in creating sources of renewable energy. The Chinese government has been investing hundreds of billions of dollars and creating millions of jobs in clean power. China has already built huge solar and wind farms, helping fuel the growth of major industries that sell their products around the world. There are over 2.5 million people who work in the solar power sector alone in China, compared with only around 260,000 in the U.S. China currently has 3.5 million people working to produce clean energy, by far the most in the world.

Coal still accounts for the largest percentage of China's energy consumption, but the government has been shutting coal mines and plans to restrict the construction of new coal-fired power plants, which together are projected to cut 1.3 million jobs in the coal industry. The government in Beijing has established a goal for clean energy to meet 20% of China's energy needs by 2030. In 2015 renewable energy sources only accounted for around 10% of total U.S. energy consumption. China has already become a major manufacturer and exporter of renewable energy technology, supplying some two-thirds of the world's solar panels. It also produces nearly half of the world's wind turbines.

Nevertheless, China still faces a major battle to further curb pollution. Concentrations of lung-damaging, ground-level ozone, caused increasingly by urban traffic congestions, are rising and need to be addressed in the country's new action plan.

The government also needs to focus on the countryside, where indoor pollution caused by direct fuel combustion is responsible for more than a third of total annual deaths. Inhaling fumes from the indoor burning of coal or biomass for cooking and heating contributes to higher rates of chronic obstructive pulmonary disease. While China has provided incentives allowing households to switch to cleaner natural gas and biogas from pigs and cattle, which has halved the number of annual deaths related to indoor burning since 1990, there are still as many as 600,000 who die from this every year.

Despite the recent efforts by the Chinese government to seriously address the issue of air pollution, the damage to the health of tens of millions of people from many years of exposure to polluted air has already occurred. More than one-third of the Chinese population still regularly breathe unhealthy air. While China has begun to deal with this major health crisis, it will be at least a few decades before the air quality in Chinese cities approaches that in the advanced nations of the West.

47

● ●

Religion

The two religious traditions of ancient China were Buddhism and Daoism (at one time transliterated as "Taoism"). Together with the humanist philosophy of Confucianism these systems of thought have been enormously influential in shaping Chinese culture. Since none of these traditions require the believer to adhere only to one or the other, it was very common in traditional China for the educated class to be Confucians when it came to their philosophy of government, Daoists when they sought escape into the natural world, and Buddhists in their beliefs concerning death and the afterlife.

Buddhism was introduced into China from India in the

first century AD but did not become widespread until the Tang dynasty in the 7th century. Buddhism taught that human beings are subject to perpetual reincarnation until they can achieve salvation by detaching themselves from all desires. The version of Buddhism that became popular and has remained so through the present day posits Heaven and Hell similar to what is found in traditional Christian belief, emphasizes ethical conduct as well as the importance of faith, and includes a belief in various Buddhist saints, with a slight similarity to those in Catholicism. The most popular of these saints is Guanyin, the Goddess of Mercy, whose devotees pray to her much as Catholics might pray to the Virgin Mary.

Daoism as a philosophy dates from the original Daoist classic book called the *Dao De Jing* ("Tao Te Ching"), whose unknown author is referred to as Lao Zi, the "Venerable Old Sage." Written in the 6th century BC it emphasized the importance of living in harmony with nature but also was intended as a philosophy of governing a kingdom. Over the centuries, however, Daoism developed into a popular religion that established a host of immortals to whom believers would pray. Unlike Buddhism, popular Daoism has no sacred texts that believers read. But like Buddhism there are priests who live in the temples and maintain them. And like Buddhism there are no regular worship services as there are for Christians, Jews, and Muslims. Believers go to the temples at any time they wish to burn incense and pray.

Confucianism is based on the teachings of the scholar Kong Qiu, known in English as Confucius, who lived from 551 to 479 BC. Many Westerners mistakenly believe Confucianism to be a religion, but it is actually a social and political philosophy. The *Lúnyǔ*, called the *Analects* in English, contains the teachings of Confucius himself. Confucius stressed the need for harmony in all social relations, whether in the family or between a ruler and his subjects. While emphasizing the need for ethical conduct, he also believed that society must be hierarchical in nature. This way of thought was viewed as very advantageous to the Chinese rulers through the centuries in preserving the social order. The books written by Confucian scholars centuries after Confucius, together with the *Analects*, became the basis of the examination system that determined who could serve as officials over the course of nearly two thousand years until it was abolished in the early 20th century.

The common people have believed for millennia in various folk religions. Although these differ by locality, they have in common a belief in a host of immortals or deities to pray to for help in various aspects of life depending on the nature of each holy figure.

Christianity and Islam both arrived in China in the 7th century. Christianity was not a widespread belief in China until the work of Western missionaries in the late 19th and early 20th centuries. When the Communists came to power in 1949 all foreign missionaries were expelled and Christian churches became government-controlled institutions.

In the early 20th century many intellectuals and reformers in China began to attack all traditional Chinese religious beliefs as superstition. When the Communist Party took over the government in 1949, it declared a policy of state atheism and prohibited the members of the Party from any religious practice while they held office. Religion was tolerated, however, until the Cultural Revolution began in 1966, when the government launched a full-blown attack against any old ideas and customs as well as anything foreign, including all religions. From 1966 until the late 1970s Buddhist and Daoist temples, Christian churches, and local shrines were often damaged or destroyed.

In 1978 the Chinese Constitution was amended to allow freedom of religion. Since that time the government has officially recognized five religions, including Buddhism, Daoism, Protestant Christianity, Catholicism, and Islam. Beginning in 2005 the government also began to protect folk religions as an important part of China's cultural heritage. Despite the persecution of the Falungong cult in the early 21st century and the recent removal of giant crosses from many churches in the city of Wenzhou, religion can be practiced in China as long as it is not seen to threaten the authority of the government.

It is difficult to produce a conclusive survey of religious belief in China for a number of reasons; the government does not allow the free dissemination of information, nearly half the population lives in rural areas across a huge country, and there is a much less clearly defined sense of religious affiliation in China than in Western countries. As a result, scholarly opinion varies widely when it comes to determining the percentage of Chinese who adhere to any particular religion.

On April 3, 2018, the News Department of the State Council of the Chinese government published a white paper that estimated that only around 200 million of China's 1.4 billion people believe in one of the five major religions practiced in China. It is estimated that around 136 million Chinese regularly go to Buddhist or Daoist temples to pray. There are approximately 38 million Protestants who attend the registered churches (the government survey does not include an equally large number of Chinese who attend house churches). There are around 20 million followers of Islam. Catholics only number approximately 6 million.

The remaining 73.5% of the population are basically atheists. Although a great number of Chinese may engage in traditional rituals to honor their ancestors and on occasion pray in Buddhist or Daoist temples, they do not necessarily believe in an omnipotent God in the way that so many people do in the West and the Middle East.

One notable development in religious practice in China has been the remarkable increase in the number of Christians after 1980, when a policy of economic and social reforms was implemented. Since then the number of Christians in China has grown by an average of 10% per year. The Pew Research Center estimated that in 2010 there were 58 million Protestants as well as millions of Catholics, together comprising around 3% of the population. That figure is in accord with the Chinese government estimate that 2–3% of the population is Christian. The Pew Research Center projects that, given the dramatic growth of Christianity in China, there will likely be as many as 160 million Chinese Christians by 2025. They even predict that by 2030 the Christian population in China could reach 247 million. That would mean that China would surpass Mexico, Brazil, and the U.S. to possess the largest Christian congregation in the world!

Major Political Leaders of the 20th and 21st centuries

 Sun Yat-sen (1866–1925), a Chinese physician, writer, philosopher, and revolutionary who was the founding father of the Republic of China and its first provisional president

 Chiang Kai-shek (1887–1975), a political and military leader who served as head of the Republic of China between 1928 and 1975, first in mainland China until 1949 and then in exile in Taiwan.

 Mao Zedong (1893–1976), a Chinese communist revolutionary who became the founding father of the People›s Republic of China, which he ruled as the Chairman of the Communist Party of China from its establishment in 1949 until his death in 1976.

 Deng Xiaoping (1904–97), the paramount leader of the People's Republic of China from 1978 until his retirement in 1989.

 Jiang Zemin (1926–), president of the PRC from 1993 to 2003.

 Hu Jintao (1942–), president of the PRC from 2003 to 2012.

 Xi Jinping (1953–), president of the PRC from 2013 to the present

48

● ●

Chinese Students in the U.S.

In spite of the souring of the relationship between the U.S. and China in recent years, the number of Chinese students coming to the United States has continued to rise. Most Americans probably have no idea just how many Chinese are studying in the U.S. today. Hint: a lot.

Roughly 370,000 students from mainland China are now enrolled in American high schools and universities, which is six times more than a decade ago. A 2016 survey conducted by a Shanghai-based research firm showed that 83% of China's millionaires were planning to send their children to school abroad, mostly to America. Ironically, the elites of a rising superpower are sending their only children to the schools of their principal economic and political rival. In 2015 alone this activity contributed $11.4 billion to the American economy, according to the Department of Commerce, which has made education into one of America's top "exports" to China.

The numbers of students from China have grown fast because of the sheer size of China's population and the rise of a wealthy class made possible by the nation's rapid economic growth over the past few decades. A degree from a college or university in the U.S. carries great weight in China. Parents also want to equip their children to succeed in a globally connected world. They recognize the importance of the U.S. and that knowledge of the international language of English is essential to success in today's world.

Chinese students accounted for nearly a third (328,547)

of the 1,043,839 international students in U.S. colleges and universities in the 2015–16 academic year. India was a distant second, with 165,918 students enrolled in American colleges and universities. In 2014 Michigan State University alone had nearly 4,000 students from China, which meant that 1 out of every 10 students was Chinese. The number of Chinese students has greatly declined since then, but other major state universities like the University of Illinois, U.S.C., Purdue, and Ohio State University also have large populations of students from China.

In addition, a growing number of Chinese teenagers have been leaving the test-driven, high-pressure world of schools in China to attend high school in the U.S. Chinese students made up more than half (43,000) of the nearly 82,000 international students enrolled in U.S. high schools in the fall of 2016. The goal of the parents of these students is to improve their children's English and to better their chances of gaining admission to a good American college (a degree from a top college or university in the U.S. is very prestigious). Also a plus is the greater freedom of the American education system, which Chinese students often credit as allowing them to be more independent and creative.

Many of the Chinese high school students live with host families, and over 95% attend private schools. This is largely because U.S. immigration law states that international students can attend public schools for only one year and must reimburse the school district. Some 58% of the visas issued for Chinese high school students in 2014 and the first three months of 2015 were for Catholic or Christian schools. Chinese students who enroll at religious institutions often have little to no knowledge of Christianity. At most only 2–3% of China's people are Christians, though estimates vary, and the state-mandated school curriculum in China emphasizes atheism, Marxism, and a scientific worldview.

Nevertheless, private Catholic and Christian high schools in the U.S., as well as institutions of higher learning, are anxious to recruit students from China who can pay full tuition, to help bolster their enrollments and add to their bottom line.

49

Are Chinese-American Restaurants Chinese?

There are over forty-five thousand Chinese restaurants in the U.S. That's more than all the McDonalds, Burger Kings, and KFCs combined. And yet only a small percentage of these Chinese-American restaurants offer very much in the way of authentic Chinese cuisine. When Americans visit China, they're often shocked to discover that the "Chinese" dishes of which they're most fond, including General Tso's Chicken, Sweet and Sour Chicken, Pepper Steak, or Shrimp with Mixed Vegetables, aren't on any of the menus in Beijing or Shanghai. That's because Chinese restaurants in America have understandably adapted the dishes they serve to meet the tastes of the average American.

China has arguably the greatest variety of dishes of any cuisine in the world. That is natural enough, given that China is the world's oldest continuous civilization and for most of human history has been home to a quarter of the world's population. Every region in that vast country has its own distinctive dishes, but it is generally acknowledged that there are eight great regional cuisines.

Most Americans are at least familiar with Cantonese cuisine, originating in Guangdong Province and Hong Kong, and noted for fine seafood dishes and rice dishes that are lightly seasoned and slightly sweet with various mild sauces. An increasing number of Americans have also become fond of Sichuan cuisine, with its spicy flavors and sauces that use lots of hot black chili peppers, garlic, ginger, and peanuts. The highly refined cuisines of Jiangsu and Zhejiang Province, however, can rarely be enjoyed in Chinese restaurants in the U.S. outside of some venues in the Chinatowns of San Francisco, Los Angeles, Chicago, and New York.

Most Chinese-American restaurants offer the exact same dishes, which are only a small fraction of those that can be enjoyed in China. Most Chinese restaurant owners in America have found it easiest to buy their menus from the same few companies that long ago produced lists of the dishes that they know most Americans will like, with such favorites as Sweet and Sour Pork, Mongolian Beef, and that most popular of all dishes in Chinese-American restaurants, General Tso's Chicken.

As Jennifer Lee says in her delightful book *The Fortune Cookie Chronicles*, you might know General Tso's Chicken as General Tsao's chicken, General Tong's chicken, General Tang's chicken, General Cho's chicken, General Chai's chicken, General Joe's Chicken, or simply General's Chicken! If the General's name were actually spelled according to the standard transliteration of pinyin now used almost everywhere in the world except Taiwan, it would be known as General Zuo's Chicken.

Americans favor chicken dishes, sweet dishes, and deep-fried foods. So the perfect answer for Chinese restauranteurs, as Jennifer Lee points out, was a crispy fried chicken in a spicy, tangy sauce that's flavored with garlic, ginger, and hot chilis. This popular dish in America cannot be found on restaurant menus in China, where the 19th-century General Zuo (to use the proper transliteration of his name) is better known for his success in squelching a major rebellion than for any association with chicken. His name was given to the dish simply because he hailed from the same province of Hunan that produced the chef who invented it.

Chef Peng had fled to Taiwan from his native Hunan Province to escape the civil war raging in China. It was in Taiwan that Chef Peng developed his spicy chicken dish, but it never became particularly popular there. Chef Peng and several other chefs in Taiwan eventually made their way to the U.S., where they opened highly successful restaurants in New York City. They introduced "General Tso's Chicken" to Americans just when Richard Nixon's visit to China in 1972 had helped create a sudden burst of interest in all things Chinese, including the food.

But at least dishes like General Tso's Chicken are much closer to authentic Chinese dishes than the chop suey and chow mein that were largely what passed as Chinese food in the America of the 1940s, '50s, and '60s. Variations of these two dishes were the only Chinese food offered in the vast majority of Chinese-American restaurants then, with cheaper versions served in school cafeterias. Chop suey (Cantonese for "miscellaneous and chopped up") consisted of some kind of meat, either chicken, beef, pork, or shrimp, and eggs, cooked quickly with vegetables such as bean sprouts, cabbage, and celery, with a sauce thickened with corn starch and served over rice. If the same hodge-podge dish was served up with dried egg noodles from a can, it was called chow mein (Cantonese for "stir-fried noodles").

By the 1970s even ordinary Chinese-American restaurants began offering dishes that were actually reasonably authentic Chinese cuisine. Kong-pao chicken (aka "Palace Chicken" or "Princess Chicken"), sweet-and-sour pork, moo goo gai pan (chicken with mushrooms in a mild white sauce), and moo-shu pork are real dishes. However, kong-pao chicken was traditionally only found in Sichuan Province, and sweet-and-sour pork and moo goo gai pan are generally only enjoyed in Guangdong (Canton) Province. The northern Chinese dish of moo-shu pork is not served with pancakes and thick, sweet hoisin sauce in China as it is in the U.S. But Americans started enjoying these more authentic dishes, albeit with new variations on a theme that included substituting chicken or shrimp for pork in sweet-and-sour and moo-shu dishes.

While Chinese-American restaurants today offer at least a modicum of fairly authentic Chinese cuisine, there are notable differences between real Chinese food and what passes for Chinese food in the U.S. One major difference is that each restaurant in China has its own distinctive menu and features local specialties, together offering literally thousands more types of dishes than can be found in Chinese-American restaurants. Another noticeable difference is that in China there is a much greater variety of vegetable dishes offered in a culture that consumes far more vegetables and much less meat than a meat-based culture like America.

In addition, you will never find dishes such as Chicken or Beef or Shrimp with Mixed Vegetables. That's because, in a group-based society like China, when people go out to eat, whether for business or with family and friends, they order for the group and share all the dishes. Each vegetable is either served separately with its own sauce, or at most is only combined with one other vegetable, as in Two Winter Delights (black mushrooms and baby bok choy). It is due to the individualistic nature of our society that Chinese-American restaurants offer dishes that take the chop suey approach by combining meat or shrimp with a medley of canned vegetables; each diner in a restaurant orders their own dishes. If a patron wants to get at least some semblance of a vegetable, it must be included in the one dish. (It should be noted, too, that to use canned bamboo shoots or baby corns in cooking is something undreamt of in China.)

Except for the fairly authentic Chinese restaurants found in Chinatowns in major cities in the U.S., almost all the dishes offered in ordinary Chinese-American restaurants are stir-fried. That excludes the huge variety of noodle dishes so popular in northern China, as well as the great many types of Chinese ravioli (*jiǎozi*), dumplings (*bāozi*), and pancakes (*bǐng*).

At the end of every meal in a Chinese-American restaurant diners are always given fortune cookies along with their bill. It may surprise many Americans to learn that fortune cookies are entirely absent from restaurants in China. These sweet little wafer-like treats with paper fortunes inserted into them actually originated in Japan in the late 18th or early 19th century. They never became widely popular in Japan, let alone China. But in the 1940s Chinese restaurant owners in San Francisco and southern California introduced their version of the cookie in their establishments.

In an American culture that loved cookies and was used to a sweet treat for dessert after every meal, the fortune cookie proved a real hit. Especially because they were offered as a free bonus and had amusing sayings or predictions embedded in them. American servicemen returning from fighting in World War II in the Pacific first stopped in coastal California, where they encountered these special treats. When they returned to their hometowns in the Midwest and on the East Coast, they started demanding fortune cookies in the Chinese restaurants there. By the late 1950s Americans were consuming as many as 250 million fortune cookies each year!

But don't expect to get one with the check in any restaurant in China.

50

American Fast Food in China

China is America's biggest trading partner, exchanging over $630 billion in goods each year. The U.S. government has expressed serious concern over the huge trade imbalance with China, in which the U.S. imports nearly $370 billion more from China than it exports. Often overlooked is that these trade numbers also mean China is the third largest market for American products, buying $130 billion of American goods in 2017. One of many areas that U.S. companies have been incredibly successful in selling their goods in China is the establishment of American fast food chains.

The spread of American fast food restaurants in China has been remarkable both for how rapidly they have sprung up in China and for the sheer number of them. According to a report from the market intelligence reporting company WorldIBIS, the fast-food industry in China generated over $150 billion in 2017, up nearly 10% from the year before. Over the past five years, industry revenue has grown at a rate of more than 11% annually, compared to only around 3% in the U.S. over that same period.

Western-style fast food in China only began to appear in China in 1987, when KFC established its first restaurant in Beijing. McDonald's followed in 1990 by opening its first outlet in Shenzhen, which was then a "Special Economic Zone" in which the Chinese could experiment with capitalism. Just a few years later, the largest McDonald's in the world opened in 1992 in Beijing. The appearance of these American restaurants reflected the fact that, after three decades of the country being closed to Western nations, China had now begun to open itself up to becoming part of the global economy.

There are now five thousand KFC franchises in 1,100 cities in China, and KFC remains the most popular of all American fast-food chains there. McDonald's currently boasts only twenty-five hundred outlets in China, but plans on opening two thousand additional restaurants, which will make China the company's second largest market after the U.S. And China is the biggest source of earnings for Yum Brands, which owns Pizza Hut and KFC. Yum recently announced plans to add more than fifteen thousand restaurants in China within the next fifteen years.

Starbucks coffee houses are now visible all over the major cities in China as well. A new Starbucks opens in China every fifteen hours, and the company said China will surpass the U.S. as its largest market within a decade.

How did American companies get to this point in a country where foreign businesses were mostly prohibited a mere forty years ago? The answer lies in a combination of timing, adaptation, and marketing ingenuity. Of course China is the world's most populous country, which has long made it an incredibly promising market for foreign companies, especially as its standard of living continues to rise so rapidly.

Because the population is largely concentrated along the eastern seaboard, including the four most important economically advanced cities of Beijing, Shanghai, Guangzhou, and Shenzhen, Western companies have focused on snapping up prime locations in those cities, particularly close to the major tourist sites. KFC's first location was on the southern edge of Beijing's Tiananmen Square, and McDonald's first outlet was a two-floor restaurant on Beijing's premiere commercial street of Wangfujing. Starbucks has an outlet near the Great Wall

of China and even had one within the Forbidden City until protests by the Chinese public against having a commercial enterprise inside such an iconic historical site forced them to move it just outside. Once these Western companies had achieved brand recognition, it became much easier to successfully open outlets in less prominent locations.

One of the major reasons American fast-food companies have been so successful in China is that Chinese food in general is also fast and convenient. Therefore the Chinese were already used to fast, cheap food. But the seemingly exotic nature of American food has made it more appealing. When restaurants like KFC and McDonald's first opened in China, for many Chinese it was their first taste of the Western world, and the experience felt just the slightest bit rebellious. Chinese families began dining there to distinguish themselves as people who dared to experience foreign culture and who had the money to do so.

Another major reason for the success of American fast-food chains is their high standard of hygiene. McDonald's and

KFC have placed a huge emphasis on cleanliness. China has only recently established regulations in regard to food, but they are rarely enforced, and the result has been that many Chinese restaurants are nowhere as sanitary as the American fast food restaurants. The Beijing media regularly praise McDonald's and KFC for their high standards of hygiene, while decrying the lack of cleanliness of their Chinese competitors. Over the years, China has become infamous for its domestic food scandals, including such things as tainted baby formula and fake eggs. Chinese consumers believe that American companies hold themselves to much higher standards than their Chinese counterparts and won't cheat them the way Chinese companies sometimes do.

Yet another factor in the success of brands like KFC has been their ability to adapt their offerings to suit Chinese taste. While still offering its signature fried chicken, KFCs in China also offer pork chops, curry, Chinese deep-fried dough sticks (油条), Chinese rice porridge, and even rather authentic Portuguese-style egg tarts.

Brands like Pizza Hut and Starbucks have succeeded in part by rebranding themselves in China. Chinese "Pizza Hut Casual Dining" emporiums are much more upscale than their counterparts in the U.S. They decorate tables with red tablecloths and offer a broad variety of pizzas, entrees, pasta, rice dishes, appetizers, beverages, and desserts. Pizza Hut is the leading Western casual dining brand in China with 1,600 restaurants in over 400 cities.

The highest Pizza Hut in the world sits on the twenty-fourth floor of a skyscraper in Xiamen, a large and prosperous city on the southeastern coast of China. Unlike in the U.S., the restaurant offers far more than just pizza. Pizza Hut in China has a full wine list and a three-course menu complete with dessert. The menu is extensive, with not only pizza and pasta, but salads, steaks, and even a brunch menu with bacon and scrambled eggs. Pizza toppings include Beijing duck and seafood. Risotto comes loaded with mushrooms, and clam chowder is served under a pastry puff cap. During their meal diners can enjoy a spectacular view of the harbor. While Pizza Hut struggles for survival in the U.S., this Pizza Hut in southeast China is a popular date-night spot that attracts couples dressed to kill.

Starbucks has also significantly rebranded itself in China. The world's largest Starbucks is located in Shanghai. The 29,000-square-foot giant structure opened in December 2017 and continues to be packed with customers. The store can serve up to seven thousand customers each day. One of the coffee bars spans 88 feet and is advertised as the longest in the world. Craft beer and nitrogen-brewed tea are readily available, and the food and baked goods they offer are produced by a famous Italian bakery.

The coffee chain is wildly successful in China, where it sells itself as an authentic taste of the West. One of the things that the Chinese love about Starbucks is that there's always a seating area. In most urban environments in China it's really difficult to find any place to sit. Starbucks provides a place where people can sit down, enjoy a coffee and snack, and chat with their friends.

One final successful marketing strategy has been employed by KFC. Knowing how urban parents in China tend to spoil their only children and accede to their every wish, KFC wanted to make their restaurants particularly appealing to children. They discovered that Chinese children were put off by the bearded, elderly white man that the chain has always used in its American outlets, so in 1995 in place of Colonel Sanders they substituted a playful cartoon character whom they named "Chicky." Other means of attracting children employed by McDonald's as well as KFC include providing play areas, child-height sinks, smaller furniture, and settings for birthday parties, the last of which is a very recent phenomenon in China.

Despite the incredible success of American fast food chains in China, there has started to be some serious competition from domestic companies. While Yum Brands, parent company of KFC and Pizza Hut, still has the greater market share, Chinese copycat competitors like Hua Lai Shi and Ting Hsin International Group, which owns the burger chain Dicos, are slowly making inroads in the market, offering similar burgers and chicken nuggets. The advantage of the Chinese chains is that they're generally cheaper and are better at offering menu items that appeal to Chinese tastes, such as fish fillet burritos, hamburger with a deep-fried shrimp patty smothered in XO sauce and sandwiched with a rice patty, and tuna salad bagels with corn.

Unfazed by the increased competition, American companies continue their expansion plans in China. Even smaller brands are entering the Chinese market. The burger chain Shake Shack, based in New York City, opened in Shanghai in early 2019. The Chinese market is simply too huge to ignore.

51

Most Chinese Don't Eat Dog Meat!

A common misperception in Western countries, including the U.S., is that the Chinese commonly eat dog meat. It doesn't help that in the past few years the Western media have widely reported on the Dog Meat Festival held in the small Chinese city of Yulin in the southern province of Guangxi. During this festival, which began in 2009 and is held for ten days at the time of the summer solstice, it is estimated that over ten thousand dogs are consumed. The festival has drawn widespread criticism both in China and across the globe. Because the eating of dog meat is a tradition of the local minority people in Yulin, the Chinese government has been reluctant to outlaw the practice.

It is true that the Chinese have used dog meat as one source of food from as early as 500 BC. Dog meat consumption has also been recorded in many parts of the world, including West Africa, Europe, and the Americas. Dog meat is still consumed in many parts of China, Korea, and Vietnam. It is especially popular in winter months, since it is believed to raise body temperature and help warm the body, and in the summer in southern climes, where it is believed to help alleviate the heat. Dog meat is also thought to have medicinal value.

Approximately 10 million dogs are killed for consumption every year in China, making it the largest consumer of dog meat in the world. In South Korea between 2 million and 2.5 million dogs are slaughtered for food each year. Vietnam butchers around 5 million dogs for consumption annually. As the populations of South Korea and Vietnam are a small fraction of the population of China, both the Koreans and the Vietnamese eat far more dog meat per capita than the Chinese.

Nevertheless, most Chinese have never tasted dog meat. Dog meat consumption in China is mostly limited to three provinces. It's most prevalent in the southern provinces of Guangdong and Guangxi, which account for approximately two-thirds of all dogs killed for meat. The other third is mostly consumed in the northeastern province of Jilin, close to Korea. It is still common enough to find dog meat served in restaurants in southeastern China, where dogs are raised on farms specifically for that purpose. Even more disturbing is that there are cases where meat from stolen pets has been discovered on menus.

Dogs have not been seen as pets in China until very recently. They were common in rural areas, where they served in part as companions but mostly as work animals, performing functions like shepherding and assisting with some of the farm labor. Although these dogs were considered useful and often given names, they generally weren't considered pets in the Western sense of the word and were also considered a potential source of food if the need for meat ever outweighed their usefulness on the farm.

Pet dogs used to be quite uncommon in Chinese cities, where they served no practical purpose because there was no farm work to be done. The rise of China's modern middle class and a shift in attitudes about animal intelligence and animal welfare has led to a sharp rise in the ownership of dogs as pets, and today dogs are a common sight on streets in Chinese cities nationwide. Dogs are the most popular pet in China, followed by cats and turtles. In a country where urban families were for decades limited to a single child and single women increasingly prefer to nest alone, dogs provide companionship. There are 62 million canines registered nationwide, and two-thirds of Chinese pet owners are thirty-five or younger, according to a recent survey done by a consulting firm in Beijing.

(Domesticated dogs very possibly originated in East Asia. There are many breeds native to China and its borderlands, from the pug, the Lhasa apso, and shih tzu ("lion dogs") to the shar pei, chow chow, and Tibetan terrier.)

The Chinese government hasn't quite caught up with the modern attitudes of its people, though, and dog lovers in China face a few issues. One is that many cities require owners to register their dogs and forbid the ownership of medium-size or large dogs. Many dogs are believed to be unregistered because fees can reach hundreds of dollars each year. Animal shelters are packed with discarded pets. To be fair, the Chinese government feels a need to respond to the widespread problem caused by hundreds of thousands of abandoned dogs who roam city streets, often biting people and infecting them with rabies.

Barring a legislative ruling one way or the other, China's tradition of dog-eating isn't going to disappear overnight. But the practice is generally frowned on by the younger generations, who have been raised with a more cosmopolitan worldview and who have experienced the joy of owning dogs as pets. Dog meat consumption is definitely declining or disappearing. In 2014 dog meat sales decreased by a third compared to the year earlier. In 2017 millions of Chinese voted in support of a legislative proposal by Zhen Xiaohe, a deputy to the National People's Congress, to ban the dog meat trade altogether.

52

High-speed Railways

In the early 1980s China was still a land where most people got around on one-speed bicycles or on foot. Three decades later, Chinese people not only buy more private automobiles per year than any other country, including the U.S., but have the world's most developed high-speed rail system.

It has all happened nearly as rapidly as the Chinese bullet trains travel. In 2007 China had no high-speed rail service at all. By 2017 it had 22,000 kilometers (14,000 miles) of high-speed rail lines, more than the rest of the world combined, with approximately two-thirds of the world's high-speed rail tracks. (High-speed rail in China is defined as railways designed for passenger trains with multiple cars to run at speeds of 250–350 kilometers per hour, or 155–217 mph.) The country is planning to lay another 15,000 kilometers by 2025.

China also boasts the Shanghai "Maglev," the world's first high-speed commercial magnetic levitation line, with trains that take passengers from Shanghai's international airport into the Pudong business district at speeds that reach 430 km per hour (267 mph).

The Chinese train network runs between all the major cities and now covers twenty-nine of the thirty-three provinces and main administrative areas. It accommodates both passenger lines and freight lines. The bullet train between

Beijing in the north and the important commercial city of Guangzhou (Canton) in the far southeast, at 2,298 km (1,428 miles), is the world's longest high-speed rail line. China's bullet trains carried more than 1.44 billion passengers in 2016, more than any other rapid train system in the world.

The railway system in China is owned and administered by the government's Ministry of Railways. By 2016 the system operated 2,595 high-speed trains, around 60% of all such trains globally. In the early years China's high-speed trains were built by foreign companies such as Siemens and Kawasaki. More recently, Chinese engineers have been manufacturing trains themselves or redesigning the older ones.

Impressive as this achievement is, the high-speed railway system in China has not been without its problems. In 2011 there was a signaling failure that resulted in the death of forty passengers. This incident caused China to lower the speed of its fastest trains from a world's fastest speed of 350 km per hour (almost 220 mph!) to a safer 300 km per hour. Since then the bullet trains have experienced few problems, and in 2017 the most important line between Beijing and Shanghai resumed running as fast as 350 km per hour.

A major concern that remains is the high cost of such an extensive system. The lines that run between the largest cities, such as the Beijing–Guangzhou line, are extremely popular and justify the cost. However, the long journeys that serve relatively sparse populations, such as in the northern and western parts of the country, have come at a huge cost to the government and resulted in large losses of revenue.

China Railway Corporation, the state-owned company that operates the train system, has debts of more than 4 trillion yuan. That amounts to around 6% of China's GDP. Not counting construction costs, six lines have at least started to operate at a profit. The Beijing–Shanghai line is the world's most profitable bullet train, bringing in 6.6 billion yuan (over

$1 billion) in 2016. But the lines that service less populated areas are incurring huge losses.

Nevertheless, China plans to continue to expand its high-speed rail system. At present it has four big north-south and east-west lines. The new plan is to have eight lines running in each of those directions, using 45,000 kilometers of high-speed track. with some Chinese engineers saying that only 5,000 kilometers will be in areas with dense enough populations to justify the tremendously high cost.

Although it has come at a high cost, the introduction of rapid train travel has helped transform Chinese society and the economy. The system serves a very wide range of riders across almost all income levels, providing Chinese business-people and ordinary travelers alike with fast, safe, convenient, and comfortable passage over large distances at an affordable price and with a much higher guarantee of punctuality than air travel.

53

China's Cashless Society

Over a thousand years ago the Chinese were the first people in the world to use paper money. They now are poised to become the first to completely stop using cash. Mobile phone payments reached 5.5 trillion in 2016, accounting for 40% of all retail purchases. That was approximately fifty times the amount of such payments in the U.S. Some 80% of supermarkets in cities like Beijing and Shanghai allow their customers to pay for everything with one of the two major mobile payment platforms, namely Alipay, owned by Alibaba, and WeChat, owned by Tencent.

In 2006 China used cash for far more purchases than did more developed economies like the U.S. and the U.K., with cash accounting for 13% of GDP compared to around 6.5% in the U.S. and as little as 3.5% in the U.K. In fact, the Chinese didn't use credit cards at all until 1985. Even now only around one-third of all Chinese have a credit card.

However, a large percentage of people in China now have a smartphone. By 2014 there were more than 480 million smartphone users, twice as many people as the adult population of the U.S.

Since most Chinese were not accustomed to using credit cards, it has proved easy for them to adapt to paying by smartphone—they didn't have to wean themselves from paying by card. Chinese consumers have discovered that making a smartphone purchase is very simple. They only need to open the app on their phone and have the code of the item scanned. And this is true whether shopping in a large mall or buying something from a street vendor. Increasingly in China all you need to take with you when leaving your apartment, besides your key, is a smartphone. Mobile payments have skyrocketed to nearly $9 trillion a year.

This new system of smartphones for all shopping is not without its problems. There is the same concern with leaks of personal information that exists with any online purchase. It also has been difficult for elderly people to adjust to the system. And for those without fast mobile Internet, it has not proved very convenient. However, if any society becomes completely cash-free in the near future, it will likely be China.

54

• •

The Internet and Social Media

As late as the 1970s, China was nearly as poor, oppressed, and isolated from the rest of the world as North Korea is today. A mere fifty years later, China now has around eight hundred million people on the Internet. And a larger percentage of its population uses social media than in the U.S., Japan, or South Korea. A McKinsey survey of nearly six thousand Chinese Internet users found that 95% of people who live in large Chinese cities have an account with at least one social media site. The users of social media in China are also far more active than those in other countries. What the survey helped reveal as well was how widespread and varied the use of social media is in China, and how different from their use in the U.S. or other countries.

China's Internet users spend more than 40% of their time online on social media, a figure that continues to rise rapidly. This enthusiasm for all things social has inspired a wide array of companies, many with tools more advanced than those in the West. For example, Chinese users were able to upload multimedia content in social media more than eighteen months before Twitter users could do so in the United States.

China's social-media users not only are more active than those of any other country but also, in more than 80% of all cases, have multiple social-media accounts. Nearly 98% of China's more than 750 million Internet users access social media through their mobile phones. Because so many Chinese are somewhat skeptical of formal institutions and authority, users disproportionately value the advice of opinion leaders in social networks compared to the U.S. and other democratic nations.

The Chinese government has blocked Twitter, Facebook, and YouTube for fear that citizens will be exposed to what it views as potentially subversive ideas from the West. However, Chinese companies have stepped into the void to provide similar services that the government does allow because it can monitor them.

Twitter has been blocked in China since it was used to organize a protest in 2009. Sina Weibo was created in its place and offers basically the same service, although you're allowed 140 *characters* to express yourself. But Sina Weibo is used differently from Twitter because the Chinese tend to mostly post things about their personal lives rather than argue about politics. This is in part due to a concern about censorship, but it also reflects a culture in which people don't tend to discuss such topics the way individuals do in a democratic country like the U.S. There are now 600 million registered users of Weibo, with 400 million active users and 184 million daily users.

Instead of WhatsApp, the Chinese use WeChat, a mobile messaging service that is relatively more private than Weibo, since the Chinese government now mandates that WeChat users register with their real names. WeChat started off as pretty much a direct copy of WhatsApp, but in recent years it's come to be used for a lot more than just messaging and calling. You can use it to pay for everything from rent and utility fees to purchases in stores, do online shopping, and play games. In 2018 WeChat reached a billion monthly users.

Instead of Facebook Messenger, the Chinese use QQ, a messenger platform owned by Tencent, the same company that owns WeChat, just as Whatsapp is owned by Facebook. QQ recently rebranded itself to focus on entertainment and subcultures among China's youth, with features similar to Snapchat, The Chinese equivalent of YouTube is Youku and is China's main site for uploading videos. It is monitored by the Chinese government, which removes anything critical of the Communist Party. Youku also streams Netflix or Amazon-style original TV shows.

Since Google is banned in China, the Chinese rely on Baidu. It provides a lot of the same services online as Google and also features Reddit-style forums called "Baidu Tieba" and a Wikipedia-style online encyclopedia. While the Internet has been a tool for democratization in other countries, in China it cannot be assumed that the Internet promotes political participation among citizens and will bring about political change. The Chinese government employs a huge number of censors who are quick to delete online postings of political dissent and to shut down any websites or blogging sites that question its policies. When individuals post content on social media platforms like WeChat that the government deems inappropriate or destructive, it is soon deleted or blocked.

More recently, the Chinese government has created a new set of rules to regulate people's political speech on social media and mobile apps. For instance, people who set up online groups or subscription accounts through mobile apps are subject to prosecution if they publish politically offensive content. As a result, instead of being a democratizing force against the government, in China the Internet has become an effective tool for the government to continue its political censorship and strengthen the current political structure. The overwhelming control that the Chinese government has over the Internet has stifled its subversive potential.

Nevertheless, Weibo, China's extremely popular Twitter equivalent, moves too fast for censors to keep up. Despite the government's attempt to block any posts it finds threatening, there are times when censorship of Weibo has been known to

relax, allowing windows of free speech, particularly in cases of breaking news. Chinese distrust of the country's traditional media, which regularly cover up food scandals and human rights violations, is leading many people to turn to Weibo for information and news.

This micro-blogging website has helped expose incidents of various criminal activity, such as intimidation of individual citizens by gangs as well as money laundering. Weibo-based stories like that of Guo Meimei, a twenty-year-old "senior official" at the state-run Red Cross Society who posted photos of her new Lamborghini and Maserati online, ignited firestorms of discussions on weightier, more sensitive, and sometimes forbidden subjects such as corruption within state-run social organizations.

Despite state censorship and political repression, social media are changing the protest landscape in China. An authoritarian government controls national media that allow no dissenting voices and regularly fail to report on incidents that may damage the government's image. Faced with Internet censorship and heavy-handed opposition tactics, freedom of expression in China has always been limited. However, there is hope for change due to the power of social media, even with all the restrictions, to enable a democratic spreading of information that had previously been unavailable to individuals in Chinese society.

One example: In 2012 citizens of the city of Shifang in southwestern Sichuan Province staged a huge demonstration to protest the construction of a large copper refinery that residents feared would poison them. Traditional media largely declined to report on the protests themselves and instead made reference to "an incident" and the rising stock price of a tear gas company, whose product was used on protestors. By contrast, there were well over 5 million posts on Weibo containing the term "Shifang" during the following four days with 400,000 of them containing images and 10,000 containing video. A similar incident occurred in Chengdu, Sichuan Province, when factory workers went on strike to demand higher wages. State media ignored the protests while social media spread the news that tear gas was being used, along with images of the protest. Eventually officials backed down and the workers received a raise.

The increasing use of social media and the rapid spread of information are putting pressure on the government that it has never felt before even as the digital revolution is gaining more and more momentum. Democratic consciousness is rising in China, and with the state pursuing an oppressive agenda, cultural change is happening from the bottom up, rather than institutionalized change from the top down.

55

●●●●●●●●●●●●●●●●●●●●●●●●●●●●●●●●●

Social Change and New Laws

The dramatic social changes over the past four decades in China have given rise to new laws and regulations that both courts and individual citizens must learn to adjust to. One such new law is the "Civilized Behavior Promotion Law" that went into effect in 2013. The law lists ten public behaviors for which violators can be fined, including "spitting in public, smoking in a non-smoking place, failing to clean up pets' excrement in public, and damaging public sanitation facilities."

An initial draft of the law outlined a broad range of fines, but there was so much public resistance that the set of fines was simplified, and violators can apply to do community service to make up half of the fee. While citizens seem to largely support the law, there is some doubt it can be effectively enforced.

Another example: dog owners in the large and highly prosperous southern city of Shenzhen who disobey a new law mandating the use of "pet restrooms" are subject to a fine equivalent to around $80. The so-called pet restrooms are open-air enclosures filled with sand, and there are hundreds of them built next to parks and alongside city walkways.

A more serious change in social patterns that has given rise to legal action and considerable public debate concerns the obligation of children to care for their elderly parents. In December 2012 the Standing Committee of the National People's Congress approved an amendment to the Law on Rights and Interests of the Elderly, originally enacted in 1996, stipulating that children should visit their aged parents "often." It states that when grown children live apart from their parents, as is more and more the case, "they should frequently visit and pay their respects." However, it is not made clear exactly how the terms "often" or "frequently" are defined, and no penalty is specified should adult children fail to comply. Nor is there any mention of how or by whom violators would be reported.

Stanley Lubman is a Senior Fellow at the Institute of East Asian Studies at U.C. Berkeley. In a *Wall Street Journal* article he wrote in 2013 entitled "Social Changes Leave China Struggling to Define Role of Law," he states that the vagueness of the amendment has understandably stirred debate in a society where rapid social change is challenging traditional expectations of filial duties toward aging parents. While the mistreatment or neglect of the elderly by their children has been a growing problem in the new China—coupled with an erosion of the traditional belief that the oldest adult son should live with his parents and care for them in their old age—there has never been any law or regulation concerning what constitutes proper "filial" behavior.

Half of the elderly in urban areas do not live with their children, due to the relatively small size of apartments in the cities. In rural areas, because so many young and middle-aged adults have left the countryside to find more lucrative work in the cities, almost 40% of the elderly no longer live with their children, who have abandoned them in their villages.

Lubman reports that litigation in China sometimes reflects pressures to meet social change. He points to a pair of fairly recent cases involving violence against women that challenge the traditional acceptance of domestic abuse.

Traditionally, physical violence in the home has always been accepted as an unfortunate part of a marriage in China, especially in rural areas. Before the economic and social reforms of the 1980s, when city residents lived in close quarters with one another, it was the responsibility of the neighborhood police to intervene by speaking to the husband to try to prevent any further abuse, and inevitably there would be concomitant social shaming. But in the modern high-rise apartment buildings in which most urban residents now live, there is no such community policing. Cases of spousal abuse must now be handled by the courts.

In one case, Kim Lee, the American wife of a well-known Chinese English teacher, was granted a divorce by a Chinese court on the grounds of domestic violence. The court also issued a three-month restraining order against the husband that was called "unprecedented" by the Chinese media. Ms. Lee brought the case to court despite police attempts to discourage her. She succeeded in her suit for divorce in part because of public pressure she created by posting on the Internet photos of the injuries inflicted by her husband. In a country that had never before publicly confronted spousal abuse, this case provoked a nationwide debate about domestic violence. By the time the court rendered its verdict, it had provoked over three million comments on Sina Weibo, China's equivalent of Twitter.

Another example to which Lubman points is the even more serious case of Li Yan, a woman in southwestern China's Sichuan province who killed her husband after suffering years of abuse and violence. Despite a large amount of evidence documenting what she had suffered, the court ruled that she had not adequately proved domestic violence and sentenced her to death. However, in an acknowledgment of the problem of domestic abuse, in 2015 the Sichuan Higher People's Court suspended the death penalty for Li Yan, commuting her sentence to life in prison with the possibility of parole.

Women in China who killed abusive spouses were once routinely executed, but as the scale of domestic violence began to be publicly known over the last few decades through the medium of the Internet, lengthy prison sentences have become the norm and have grown lighter over time.

The cases here are examples of how changes in social values are reflected in new laws reacting to those changes. As Lubman outlines, the Shenzhen law regarding dog owners reveals limits on the influence of laws and regulations on the behavior of citizens. The new legal provisions to impose a duty on adult children to care for their elderly parents illustrate the intent of the government to encourage the preservation of certain traditional moral values in a society that has recently undergone dramatic changes in lifestyles and attitudes. And the issue of domestic violence reflects social pressures for there to be new laws to protect wives from violent husbands, while also raising doubt about the extent to which such laws would actually protect them.

Lubman concludes his *Wall Street Journal* article by saying that the power of social media will affect the outcome of litigation, and so might any meaningful increase in the independence of the courts. Pressures from society for change could affect the ruling party's current dominance over both the content of legislation and the work of the courts. Such outcomes seemed impossible for judges and lawmakers not long ago, but Chinese society is hurtling into a new era and grasping for new rules as it goes.

56

The Arts and Western Classical Music

Americans and other people in Western countries may be surprised to learn how vibrant the arts have become in contemporary China. Only four decades ago, during the Cultural Revolution (1966–76), all art was required to serve political and propaganda purposes. All Western art was banned as a decadent bourgeois foreign import and anti-revolutionary, including literature, fine arts, and classical music. The traditional Chinese arts were considered remnants of the old "feudalist" society and were also condemned by the government. In the late 1960s a mere eight "revolutionary operas" were largely the only music or theater that Chinese people ever heard or saw, beyond the songs of the revolution that all school children were required to memorize and sing.

One result of the economic and social reforms over the past forty years has been a resurgence of artistic activity. The writer Mo Yan has gained a literary reputation for his novels and short stories and received the Nobel Prize for Literature in 2012. Other writers such as Shi Tiesheng, Wang Shuo, and Yu Hua have also won international attention over the past several decades.

The artist and activist Ai Weiwei has become renowned in the West for his extensive body of work. Yet he is just one of many contemporary artists whose work has helped in shaping a post–Cultural Revolution art scene since China opened its doors to the world in the late 1970s.

It is in the realm of Western classical music that China has not only seen an explosion of artistry within its borders but has been exporting its homegrown talent across the globe. There may be no place in the world where the great works of the Western classical music tradition are so widely admired as in China. It is estimated that there are as many as forty million Chinese children studying the piano, more than six times the number of American children learning to play.

China now makes 4 out of 5 five pianos in the world today. The world's largest piano factory, the Pearl River Piano factory, is located in Guangzhou. It produces 290 pianos every day. The company was founded in 1956, and its pianos rank in quality with those made by Steinway and other famous manufacturers. Gibson, the maker of Gibson guitars and Baldwin pianos, took over Dongbei Piano Group, China's third-largest piano maker, more than a decade ago.

China has also become a major manufacturer of Western musical instruments besides pianos. It produces the overwhelming majority of the world's student-level violins, violas, cellos, and string basses. It is estimated that one million violins are produced by hundreds of factories in China each year and that 70% to 80% of all violins sold to U.S. music students are Chinese made. These range from basic student models to concert quality instruments.

The Chinese government, which only several generations ago severely punished anyone playing or listening to Mozart or Beethoven, has been spending huge amounts of money building impressive new concert halls such as the National Center for the Performing Arts in Beijing and the Shanghai Opera House.

Western classical music was introduced to the Chinese by Christian missionaries in the late 19th century, and it quickly gained popularity and prestige as a symbol of Western culture that modeled scientific progress and modernization. The rigors of classical training reflected the traditional Confucian value of self-cultivation through self-discipline. The most respected Chinese sage of all time, Confucius, believed that the study of music was a superior way to train the mind and considered music more important than mathematics and writing.

Since the end of the Cultural Revolution in 1976, both Confucius and classical music have become celebrated once again. By the early 1990s, the Chinese government was deliberately encouraging the study of music through its educational policies. Knowledge of Beethoven and Tchaikovsky became something to be prized: the Chinese president from 1993 to 2003, Jiang Zemin, liked to show off by taking up the baton to conduct orchestras at state banquets and playing the piano for Western leaders.

It is highly ironic that China's passion for Western classical music may ensure its future at a time when in the West it is seen as a high-brow entertainment for an elite few and is far overshadowed by the popular music industry. Western classical music is heard in concert halls all across China, performed by leading orchestras from Europe and the U.S., as well as by a growing number of Chinese orchestras. It is also studied at top-notch music conservatories in cities like Beijing, Shanghai, and Xian, which every year turn out young classical musicians who go on to enter the finest music schools and join the premiere orchestras in the West. The Sichuan Conservatory, in the southwestern city of Chengdu, is reported to have more than ten thousand students. The renowned Juilliard School of Music in New York has but eight hundred.

Ensembles like the China National Traditional Orchestra have been created in the image of the Western symphony orchestra to promote the country's "traditional" music culture. Chinese virtuosos and composers are prominent in the international music scene, and Western critics regularly declare that the future of classical music lies in China.

The passion for learning the piano in China is fueled at least in part by the success on the worldwide stage of two great Chinese solo pianists, Lang Lang and Yundi Li. Lang Lang's highly flamboyant manner of playing, in addition to his prodigious technique, has earned him close to rock-star status and made him very possibly the highest-earning classical musician in the world. Yundi Li, winner of the 2000 Warsaw Chopin Competition, has focused more on performing in China, where he has gained an army of teenage fans for his recitals of the great piano works of Beethoven, among other classical composers.

The Chinese are not just interested in the piano, by any means. Regional orchestras are springing up all over the country, funded by the same Communist Party that banned Western classical music only fifty years ago. Both Beijing and Shanghai hold major violin competitions. Chinese conservatories are producing top-level musicians, particularly string players. The orchestras of Beijing, Shanghai, and Hong Kong, each bolstered by a dozen or more European players, are nearing a world-class level of performance.

The most astounding phenomenon that has accompanied the explosion of classical music in China is the great number of highly talented musicians who were trained in China but who have been gaining spots in the top music schools in the West and winning positions in the best orchestras all across the U.S. and Europe.

The Chicago Symphony, long recognized as one of the five top orchestras in America, currently includes among its members eight violinists and five violists from China, including the Assistant Principal Violist, as well as their Assistant Principal Clarinetist. Another of the top five American orchestras, the Philadelphia Orchestra, now has a total of six

Chinese violinists, including their Associate Concertmaster, five Chinese violists, including their Principal Viola, with the Principal Cello also hailing from China. The Philadelphia Orchestra now spends several weeks each summer doing a residency in China, with a week each in Beijing and Shanghai.

Every ranking music conservatory in the U.S. and Europe has been marketing itself in China since demand for university degrees in music performance has fallen in the West as students seek better-paying professions. Directors of American and European music schools and conservatories fly to China twice a year to recruit students. Faced with maintaining eighty music schools that they cannot hope to fill with its own citizens, Germany now offers universal free tuition to Chinese students.

It might be said that the least-known major import into the U.S. from China these days is the wave of talented young Chinese classical musicians entering our schools and joining our orchestras. They are not only adding to the quality of musical performance in the U.S. but are assuring the future of classical music for many decades to come.

57

Wildlife in China

China may have some of the largest and most crowded cities in the world, but it also has many places of great natural beauty where a multitude of wildlife still survive. China has some of the greatest diversity of wildlife in the world. It is

home to more than 7,500 species of mammals, birds, reptiles, amphibians, and fishes, 10% of the world's total. This includes 4,936 different fish, 1,269 birds, 562 mammals, and 403 reptiles. China ranks third in the world in mammals, eighth in birds, and seventh in reptiles. There are more than 100 wild animal species unique to China, including such well-known rare animals as the giant panda, golden-haired monkey, South China tiger, brown-eared pheasant, red-crowned crane, red ibis, white-flag dolphin, and Chinese alligator.

The black-and-white giant panda weighs on average close to 300 pounds and lives on tender bamboo leaves and bamboo shoots. It is extremely rare, with fewer than 2,000 left, and has become the symbol of the world's protected wild animals. Only about 1,600 live in the wild (80% in Sichuan Province in the southwest) along with about 300 in captivity in Chinese breeding centers and zoos. The giant panda's diet is over 90% bamboo shoots. Its black and white coloring provides a degree of camouflage in the dense forests, but the adult animal has no natural predators.

Giant pandas are extremely difficult to breed. They have short mating periods and give birth to only one or two cubs per year. The giant panda cub is the smallest baby, compared to the size of the parents, of any mammal. The giant panda is considered to be a national treasure of China and as an endangered species is protected by law. Since the 1970s, giant pandas have been given or lent to foreign zoos as a token of goodwill.

Other animals unique to China include the red-crowned crane, as tall as 3½ feet, covered with white feathers, and with a striking patch of red skin on the top of its head. This crane is regarded as a symbol of long life in East Asia. The white-flag dolphin is one of only two species of freshwater whales in the world. In 1980, a male white-flag dolphin was caught for the first time in the Yangtze River, sparking great interest among dolphin researchers worldwide.

Unfortunately wildlife in China suffers greatly from having to share space with the world's largest population of humans, who have already destroyed much of their habitat. At least 840 animal species are threatened or in danger of extinction in China, due mainly to human activity such as habitat destruction, pollution, and poaching for food, fur, and ingredients for traditional Chinese medicine. On a positive note, endangered wildlife are protected by law, and as of 2005, the country has over 2,349 nature reserves, covering a total area of 578,960 square miles—about 15% of China's total land area

In addition to the world's largest population of humans, China is also home to a dozen other primate species including gibbons, macaques, leaf monkeys, and snub-nosed monkeys. Unlike human beings, who number over 1.4 billion, most of China's other primate species are endangered. Both apes and monkeys, particularly gibbons and macaques, are prominently featured in Chinese culture, folk religion, art and literature. The monkey is one of the twelve animals of the Chinese zodiac.

China's big cat species include the tiger, leopard, snow leopard, and clouded leopard. Like the monkey, the tiger is also one of the twelve animals of the Chinese zodiac and figures prominently in Chinese culture and history. Sadly, tiger bones are used in traditional Chinese medicine, and tiger fur is used for decoration, so the animal is vulnerable to poaching and habitat loss. Four tiger subspecies are native to China. All are critically endangered, protected, and live in nature reserves.

China also is home to the gray wolf, red fox, Tibetan sand fox, and raccoon dog. There are two varieties of gray wolf in China—the Eurasian wolf, found across Xinjiang, Inner Mongolia, and Heilongjiang in the northern border areas of the country, and the Tibetan wolf, which lives on the Tibetan Plateau. Some of the earliest dogs may have been domesticated in East Asia. Several Chinese dog breeds including the sharpei and chow are among the most ancient, with DNA most similar to the gray wolf's.

Asian elephants once roamed a large area of China but are now only found in two areas of southern Yunnan Province, close to Laos and Myanmar. In recent years, Chinese demand for ivory has led to a sharp increase in elephant poaching around the world. Thanks to strict enforcement of elephant-protection laws (with the death penalty for poachers) and government-funded feeding programs, the population of elephants within China from 1994 to 2014 roughly doubled to nearly three hundred—still a pathetically small number, of course.

China has a great variety of deer and musk deer. The largest deer relative is the moose, which is found in the forests of the far northeast. The moose stands over 6 feet tall and weighs as much 1,400 pounds. In contrast, the mouse-deer of

Yunnan, which is just 1½ feet in height and weighs 4 pounds, is not much bigger than a rabbit.

The grasslands, plateaus, and deserts of northern and western China are home to several species of antelope. The Mongolian gazelle, also known as the yellow sheep, can run at speeds of up to 50 mph and gathers in herds by the thousands.

There are bears in China, which include the Asiatic black bear and the brown bear, found across much of the country.

It is encouraging to note how many wonderful and fascinating animals still survive in a country with over 18% of the world's population. Nevertheless, so many natural habitats for wild animals in China have been developed for humans over the centuries that far too little wildlife habitat still remains. Fortunately with China's new prosperity, widespread education, and increased contact with the Western world, the Chinese are more and more interested in preserving what natural beauty and wild animal habitats are left.

58

China's Top Spots for Scenic Beauty

It should come as no surprise that China, a huge country almost equal in size to the United States, should have at least an equal number of places of exceptional natural beauty. When most Americans picture China, they see crowded and often polluted cities. However, much of the country contains spectacular scenery and only recently has begun to attract the attention of foreign tourists. Here is a list of ten of China's most extraordinary scenic sites.

1. Guilin and Yangshuo

The strange but beautiful karst mountain formations along the Li River that flows between the small city of Guilin and the town of Yangshuo tops everyone's list of scenic attractions in China. The mountains along the river here have inspired many centuries of Chinese landscape paintings and have appeared in many movies about China. The area is rich with scenic beauty, including some famous limestone caves and the incredibly beautiful terraced rice fields of Longji. The small town of Yangshuo downriver from Guilin is much more secluded and famous for its breathtaking natural beauty, nestled as it is alongside the Li River and surrounded by uniquely shaped mountains.

2. Huangshan (The Huang Mountains)

The Huang Mountains are a mountain range in southern Anhui Province in eastern China. The area is well known for its scenery, which abounds with peculiarly shaped granite peaks and picturesque pine trees. The mountains are a frequent subject of traditional Chinese paintings and literature. One of the best parts of visiting this nature reserve is that it can only be reached by cable car or by climbing up the slopes. No vehicles are allowed, so this is one place in China where you can escape the congestion, pollution, and noise of traffic, and wonder at nature's beauty and majesty.

3. Wulingyuan National Park in Zhangjiajie

This national park is a scenic and historical interest area in the small city of Zhangjiajie in Hunan Province. It's justly famous for its approximately 3,100 tall quartzite sandstone pillars, some of which are over 2,500 feet in height. These

strange-shaped but majestic rock formations in a lush sub-tropical setting were the inspiration for the landscapes in the movie *Avatar*. Unfortunately, few Western tourists ever visit Wulingyuan, with no more than several hundred American visitors a year and even fewer from places like England or Canada.

4. *Jiuzhaigou National Park*

Jiuzhaigou Valley is a nature reserve located in China's Sichuan Province. A beautiful example of China's varied landscape, Jiuzhaigou is famous for crystal blue lakes and multi-tiered waterfalls. It is populated by a number of Tibetan villages, so it's also a great place to see and experience Tibetan local culture.

5. *The Three Gorges*

Best seen by tour boat down the Yangtze River, these three gorges in Hubei Province are nearly 120 miles long and cover an area of over 450 square miles. Due to its magnificent scenery the Three Gorges has long been a source of inspiration for poets and artists. The Three Gorges area contains many different ecological environments and has abundant species of wildlife. Three Gorges Dam is a modern construction marvel. It is the world's largest dam as well as the world's largest hydroelectric power station. The river itself is the world's third longest, and the Three Gorges are the natural highlight of the boat cruise.

6. West Lake in Hangzhou

This scenic lake in the lovely city of Hangzhou is surrounded by mountains on three sides and has an area of around 2 square miles. The circumference is around 9 miles, along which there are a great many beautiful gardens and pagodas. West Lake is not only famous for its picturesque landscape but is also associated with many famous historical figures. Its ancient buildings, stone caves, and engraved tablets in surrounding areas are among the most cherished national treasures of China.

7. Wuyi Mountains

The Wuyi Mountains, located in China's southeast province of Fujian, feature uniquely shaped mountains overlooking the dramatic gorges of the Nine Bend River. There are numerous ancient temples and monasteries situated along the river. The river rafting tours are one of the main tourist attractions. This extensive and unspoiled area contains the largest, most representative example of a largely intact forest encompassing the biodiversity of a Chinese subtropical rainforest.

8. Mt. Emei in Sichuan Province

At 10,000 feet, Mt. Emei is the tallest and arguably most beautiful of the Four Sacred Buddhist Mountains of China. It is also notable for its exceptionally diverse vegetation, ranging from subtropical to subalpine pine forests. Some of the trees here are more than a thousand years old. There are many cultural treasures in the area, most remarkable of which is the Giant Buddha at Leshan. Carved out of the cliff face and standing well over 200 feet high, it guards the place where three rivers come together at its feet and is the tallest Buddha in the world.

9. Tiger Leaping Gorge and the Ancient Village of Lijiang

Over 10 miles in length, this gorge in Yunnan Province is located where a river passes between the 18,000-foot-high Jade Dragon Snow Mountain and the almost equally high Haba Snow Mountain in a series of rapids under steep 6,000-foot cliffs. Legend says that in order to escape from a hunter, a tiger jumped across the river at the narrowest point (over 75 feet wide!), hence the name.

Tiger Leaping Gorge is one of the world's deepest river canyons. The inhabitants of the gorge are primarily the native Naxi people, who live in a handful of small villages. It's possible to hike the length of the gorge. The hiking path is well maintained and marked, although sometimes narrow, and is used by the natives in their everyday life. The trail features a variety of small ecosystems, waterfalls, and guesthouses for hikers.

Nearby is the lovely and quaint ancient village of Lijiang. The city has an eight-hundred-year history. It is built where the Jade River divides into three, its streams forming the canals and waterways that flow along the old town streets. When you ascend to the park above the village, you can see majestic mountains in the distance, including Jade Dragon Snow Mountain.

10. Himalayas in Tibet

The Himalayas form the highest plateau in the world with an average elevation of more than 16,000 feet. No wonder it is also called the Roof of the World. The Chinese part of the Himalayas is in the Autonomous Region of Tibet. The breathtakingly beautiful Trans-Himalayan drive of 600 miles takes you through four mountainous passes and offers a panoramic view of scenery and of the Tibetan way of life.

59

China's Emerging Role in the World

From 1949 when the Communist Party gained control of China until the economic and social reforms begun in the late 1970s, China was one of the poorest and most isolated of countries in the world. In a mere four decades the country has risen to challenge the United States as a major economic rival. Since the end of World War II until the present day, the U.S. with its democratic institutions and free-market economy seemed to provide the best model for developing nations across the globe to follow. But the emergence of China on the world stage as a major power has somewhat changed that view.

As Ian Bremmer, the American political scientist, points out in his article entitled "How China's Economy Is Poised to Win the Future," which appeared in the November 13, 2017, edition of *Time* magazine, the Chinese authoritarian-capitalist model of an authoritarian state that combined a socialist economy with capitalist free enterprise was not predicted to survive, let alone thrive, in a global free market. Until very recently the general consensus was that China would eventually need major democratic reforms to maintain its legitimacy and that the country could not possibly sustain its state-run capitalist economic system.

However, at the present moment it is China's political and economic system that appears better equipped and perhaps even more sustainable than the American model. While the U.S. economy still remains the world's largest, China's ability to use state-owned companies to carry out the Party's directives in both domestic and foreign economic initiatives ensures that the rising superpower will very possibly surpass the U.S. in GDP by 2029, according to the Center for Economics and Business Research.

The U.S. still exerts the greatest influence in today's world: The GDP of the U.S. is at present almost equal to the combined GDP of the next three largest economies of China, Japan, and Germany, and the U.S. dollar will like remain the global reserve currency well into the future. English will continue to be the lingua franca for the world, not Chinese. Wealthy Chinese continue to invest in U.S. real estate and send their kids to U.S. high schools and universities. But as Bremmer puts it, "the foundation of U.S. power, including its military alliances, its leadership in world trade, and its willingness to promote Western political and moral values, is weakening."

At the same time, the leaders of other emerging powers, from authoritarian Russia to democratic nations such as India and Turkey, are following China's lead in creating systems where the government encourages international trade while tightly controlling politics, economic competition, and the flow of information. This process has been occurring for many years. However, China now has its strongest leader in decades, while the U.S. has a leader who, as of this writing, is committed to having his country withdraw from many of its international partnerships and to abandoning its leadership role in the "free world." Bremmer questions whether Americans and Europeans were correct in always assuming that "the long arc of human development bends toward liberal democracy."

As a sign of China's new global ambitions, Chinese President Xi Jinping recently announced his Belt and Road Initiative, an incredibly ambitious plan to build a network of highways, railways, and pipelines linking Asia via the Middle East to Europe and south through Africa. The economic land "belt" takes cargo through Eurasia. A maritime "road" links coastal Chinese cities via a series of ports to Africa and the Mediterranean. A total of nine hundred separate projects have been earmarked at a cost of $900 billion, according to the China Development Bank. They include a $480 million deep-sea port in Kenya, which will eventually be connected via road, railway, and pipeline to landlocked South Sudan and Ethiopia and right across Africa to Cameroon's port of Douala. Also proposed is a new $7.3 billion pipeline from Turkmenistan that will bring China an additional 15 billion cubic meters of gas each year.

As Charlie Campbell states in his October 2017 article in *Time* magazine, the Belt and Road initiative represents a vision of connections across the globe that will make China a prominent leader on the international stage at a time when the U.S. is wavering in its international commitments. China's expansive undertaking will connect as many as sixty-five countries. It will link 70% of the planet's population, include 75% of its energy resources, and cover 25% of goods and services and 28% of global GDP amounting to over $20 trillion. The Chinese government's rationale for the project is that these are large, resource-rich nations in great need of improved infrastructure, and China has the resources and the expertise to provide that. More to the point is that the Belt and Road initiative will allow China to gain access to valuable natural resources and establish new and promising markets for its goods far into the future.

After spending most of the 20th century suffering from foreign invasion, devastating wars, poverty, and political turmoil, China feels it is now assuming its rightful position as the most populous nation in the world and the second largest economy. China has produced the most solar panels, wind turbines, and high-speed rail of any country in the world. In January of 2018, when Chinese President Xi became the first Chinese leader to address the World Economic Forum in Davos, he appeared as a confident, responsible statesman with a global perspective who could help establish international rules of trade and environmental standards.

In stark contrast, the U.S. has been having trouble passing a $1 trillion infrastructure plan to rebuild the nation's crumbling roads, bridges, and electricity grid, despite the general consensus that such an initiative is urgently needed. America's withdrawal from the Trans-Pacific Partnership trade agreement has weakened the U.S. as a major player in the economy of the Pacific region. And President Trump's tariffs imposed on goods from our major trading partners, including our allies, has antagonized Canada, Mexico, and the EU countries. America's withdrawal from the Paris Climate Accord has left the world looking to China for leadership on this and other issues.

Those of us who are so fortunate as to live in a democratic nation like the U.S. or Canada would never wish to live in an authoritarian state like China. Political repression and the lack of rule of law in China create injustice at every level of society. Nevertheless, the reality is that the leader of a government like China's can simply provide direct financial support to strategic industries and prop up any that may be failing in a way that a democratic government cannot. China has contributed sizable amounts of cash to the country's three largest oil companies via state-owned banks, for example. In an era when automation has caused the loss of millions of manufacturing jobs in developed countries like the U.S., the Chinese government's control of the economy allows it to protect jobs or retrain workers far beyond anything democratic governments might be able to manage.

Ian Bremmer points out that China's most important ambitions are in artificial intelligence. Bremmer calls this "the space race of the 21st century, but one with a much more direct impact on the lives and livelihoods of citizens." The Chinese government is making a long-term commitment to investing in AI, while the U.S. government is leaving such development to the private companies in Silicon Valley. Bremmer cautions that our democratic and free-market capitalist systems may not be able to compete with the Chinese in the competition for superiority in AI.

It remains uncertain whether China can successfully challenge the position of the U.S. as the world's most powerful nation any time in the near future. And as Bremmer concludes in his 2017 article in *Time* magazine, "no one government will have the international influence required to continue to set the political and economic rules that govern the global system." But China presents an alternative economic and political model that the West was certain would eventually fail. And yet it has defied all expectations to raise an impoverished and isolated nation to the #2 economy in the world. China will most definitely continue to be a major player on the world stage in the decades to come and is the only nation that can come close to rivaling the U.S. in power and influence over the course of this century.

Bibliography

"A History of Tea." mightyleaf.com.

Adler, Joseph A. "Chinese Religion: An Overview." In Lindsay Jones, *Encyclopedia of Religion*, 2nd ed. Detroit: Macmillan Reference USA, 2005.

"After the Cultural Revolution: What Western Classical Music Means in China." *Guardian*, July 8, 2016.

Armedforces.edu.

Asiapac Editorial Board. *Origin of Chinese Names*. Singapore: Asiapac, 2008.

Banister, Judith. *A Brief History of China's Population, The Population of Modern China*. Palo Alto: Stanford University Press, 1991.

Baumler, Alan. *Modern China and Opium: A Reader*. Ann Arbor: University of Michigan Press, 2001.

Beckwith, Christopher I. *Empires of the Silk Road: A History of Central Eurasia from the Bronze Age to the Present*. Princeton: Princeton University Press, 2009.

Bodde, Derk (1986). "The State and Empire of Ch'in." In Denis Twitchett and Michael Loewe, The Cambridge History of China, volume I: *The Ch'in and Han Empires, 221 B.C.-A.D. 220.* Cambridge: Cambridge University Press, 1986.

Bradley, James. *The China Mirage: The Hidden History of American Disaster in Asia*. New York: Little, Brown, and Company, 2015.

Bremmer, Ian. "How China's Economy Is Poised to Win the Future." *Time*, November 13, 2017.

Brook, Timothy, and Bob Tadashi Wakabayashi. *Opium Regimes: China, Britain, and Japan, 1839-1952*. Berkeley: University of California Press, 2000.

Burton, William. *Porcelain, Its Nature, Art and Manufacture*. London: Batsford, 1906.

Campbell, Charlie. "Ports, Pipelines, and Geopolitics: China's New Silk Road Is a Challenge for Washington." *Time*, October 23, 2017.

Carter, Peter. *Mao*. London: Oxford University Press, 1976.

Carter, Thomas Frances. *The Invention of Printing in China, and Its Spread Westward*. 2nd ed., revised by L. Carrington Goodrich. New York: Ronald Press, 1955 (1st ed., 1925).

Cassel, Susan Lan. *The Chinese in America: A History from Gold Mountain to the New Millennium*. Lanham, MD: AltaMira Press, 2002.

Chang, Iris. *The Chinese in America: A Narrative History*. New York: Penguin, 2004.

Chang, Jung, and Jon Halliday. *Mao: The Unknown Story*. London: Jonathan Cape, 2005.

China Ethnic Statistical Yearbook, 2016

Cotterell, Yong Yap, and Arthur Cotterell. *The Early Civilization of China*. New York: G. P. Putnam's Sons, 1975.

Davin, Delia. *Mao: A Very Short Introduction*. Oxford: Oxford University Press, 2013.

Dikötter, Frank. *Mao's Great Famine: The History of China's Most Devastating Catastrophe, 1958–62*. London: Walker and Company, 2010.

Dong, Lan. *Mulan's Legend and Legacy in China and the United States*. Philadelphia: Temple University Press, 2010.

Dreyer, Edward L. *Zheng He: China and the Oceans in the Early Ming, 1405–1433*. Library of World Biography. London: Longman, 2007.

Fairbank, John King. *China: A New History*. Cambridge, MA: Belknap Press/Harvard University Press, 1992.

——— and Merle Goldman. *China: A New History*. Cambridge, MA: Harvard University Press, 2006.

Feigon, Lee. *Mao: A Reinterpretation*. Chicago: Ivan R. Dee, 2002.

Fenby, Jonathan. *Generalissimo Chiang Kai-Shek and the China He Lost*. New York: Free Press, 2003.

Finlay, Robert. *The Pilgrim Art: Cultures of Porcelain in World History*. California World History Library (illustrated ed.), volume 11. Berkeley: University of California Press, 2010.

Fish, Eric. *China's Millennials: The Want Generation*. Lanham, MD: Rowman and Littlefield Publishers, 2015.

Gladney, Dru C. "Representing Nationality in China: Refiguring Majority/Minority Identities." *Journal of Asian Studies*, 1994

Gray, Jack. *Rebellions and Revolutions: China from the 1800s to 2000*. Oxford: Oxford University Press, 1990.

Greenberg, Michael. *British Trade and the Opening of China, 1800–42*. Cambridge Studies in Economic History. Cambridge: Cambridge University Press, 1969.

Guo, Sujian. *Chinese Politics and Government: Power, Ideology and Organization*. London and New York: Routledge, 2012.

Hanes, W. Travis, and Frank Sanello. *Opium Wars: The Addiction of One Empire and the Corruption of Another*. Napierville, IL: Sourcebooks, 2002.

Heath, Ian. *The Taiping Rebellion, 1851–1866*. Osprey Military Men-at-Arms Series. London and Long Island City: Osprey, 1994.

Herzberg, Larry. *Speak and Read Chinese: Fun Mnemonic Devices for Remembering Chinese Words and Their Tones*. Berkeley, CA: Stone Bridge Press, 2016.

——— and Qin Herzberg. *China Survival Guide: How to Avoid Travel Troubles and Mortifying Mishaps*. 3rd ed. Berkeley, CA: Stone Bridge Press, 2013.

——— and Qin Herzberg. *Chinese Proverbs and Popular Sayings: With Observations on Culture and Language*. Berkeley, CA: Stone Bridge Press, 2012.

Hou, Lixian. *LGBT Activism in Mainland China*. "Solidarity" Newsletter, November-December, 2014.

Hsu, Immanuel C. Y. *The Rise of Modern China*. New York and Oxford: Oxford University Press, 1999.

Jian, Youwen. *The Taiping Revolutionary Movement*. New Haven: Yale University Press, 1973.

Jiang, Cheng An. *Empress of China: Wu Ze Tian*. Monterey, CA: Victory Press, 1998.

Jones, Gareth. "The Cashless Society Has Arrived—Only It's in China." *Wall Street Journal,* January 19, 2018.

Kahn, Joseph, and Daniel Wakin. "Western Classical Music, Made and Loved in China." *New York Times*, April 2, 2007.

Kwa, Shiamin, and Wilt L. Idema. *Mulan: Five Versions of a Classic Chinese Legend with Related Texts.* Indianapolis: Hackett Publishing, 2010.

Lai, Him Mark. *Becoming Chinese American. A History of Communities and Institutions.* Lanham, MD: AltaMira Press, 2004.

Layton, Thomas N. *The Voyage of the "Frolic": New England Merchants and the Opium Trade.* Palo Alto: Stanford University Press, 1999.

Lee, Jennifer. *The Fortune Cookie Chronicles: Adventures in the World of Chinese Food.* New York: Twelve, 2008.

Leibovitz, Liel, and Matthew I. Miller. *Fortunate Sons: The 120 Chinese Boys Who Came to America, Went to School, and Revolutionized an Ancient Civilization.* New York: Norton, 2011.

Levathes, Louise. *When China Ruled the Seas: The Treasure Fleet of the Dragon Throne, 1405–1433.* Oxford: Oxford University Press, 1996.

Levy, Howard S. *The Lotus Lovers: The Complete History of the Curious Erotic Tradition of Foot Binding in China.* New York: Prometheus Books, 1991.

Lewis, Mark Edward. *The Early Chinese Empires: Qin and Han.* London: Belknap Press, 2007.

Littlejohn, Ronnie. *Confucianism: An Introduction.* London: I. B. Tauris, 2010.

Liu, Xinru. *The Silk Road in World History.* Oxford: Oxford University Press, 2010.

Lockie, Alex. "How the World's Largest Military Stacks up to the US Armed Forces." *Business Insider*, August 5, 2016.

Lovell, Julia. *The Great Wall: China Against the World.* New York: Grove Press, 2007.

Lubman, Stanley. "Social Changes Leave China Struggling to Define Role of Law." *Wall Street Journal*, February 27, 2013.

Mair, Victor H., and Erling Hoh. *The True History of Tea.* London: Thames and Hudson, 2009.

Maurer-Fazio, M., and R. Hasmath. "The Contemporary Ethnic

Minority in China: An Introduction." *Eurasian Geography and Economics* 56(1): 1–7, 2015.

McGregor, Richard. *The Party: The Secret World of China's Communist Rulers.* 2nd ed. New York: Harper Perennial, 2012.

Menzies, Gavin. *1421: The Year China Discovered America.* New York: William Morrow, 2003.

Miyazaki, Ichisada. *China's Examination Hell: The Civil Service Examinations of Imperial China.* New York and Tokyo: Weatherhill, 1976.

Murck, Alfreda. *Poetry and Painting in Song China: The Subtle Art of Dissent.* Cambridge, MA, and London: Harvard University Asia Center for the Harvard-Yenching Institute, 2000.

National Bureau of Statistics of China.

Paludan, Ann. *Chronicle of the Chinese Emperors: The Reign-by-Reign Record of the Rulers of Imperial China.* New York: Thames and Hudson, 1998.

Pfaelzer, Jean. *Driven Out: The Forgotten War Against Chinese Americans.* New York: Random House, 2007.

Ping, Wang. *Aching for Beauty: Footbinding in China.* New York: Anchor Books, 2002.

Pulleyblank, E. G. "The An Lu-Shan Rebellion and the Origins of Chronic Militarism in Late T'ang China." In John Curtis and Bardwell Smith, *Essays on T'ang Society.* Leiden: E. J. Brill, 1976.

———. *The Background of the Rebellion of An Lu-Shan.* London: Oxford University Press, 1955.

Shambaugh, David. *China's Communist Party: Atrophy and Adaptation.* Berkeley: University of California Press, 2008.

Short, Philip. *Mao: A Life.* Owl Books, 2001.

"Silk." *Encyclopedia Britannica.* Chicago: Encyclopedia Britannica, 2008.

Silva, Cristina. "What China's Military Looks Like Compared to the U.S." *Newsweek*, November 7, 2017.

Spence, Jonathan, D. *The Search for Modern China.* New York: Norton, 1999.

———. *God's Chinese Son: The Taiping Heavenly Kingdom of Hong Xiuquan.* New York: W. W. Norton, 1996.

Su, Ming-Yang. *Seven Epic Voyages of Zheng He in Ming China, 1405–1433: Facts, Fiction and Fabrication.* Self-published, 2004.

Taylor, Jay. *The Generalissimo: Chiang Kai-shek and the Struggle for Modern China.* Cambridge, MA: Belknap Press/Harvard University Press, 2009.

"Tea." *Encyclopedia Britannica.* Chicago: Encyclopedia Britannica, 2008.

"The History of Tea by Twinings." Twinings.uk.com.

Tsai, Shih-Shan Henry. *The Chinese Experience in America.* Bloomington, IN: Indiana University Press, 1986.

Tsien, Tsuen-Hsuin. *Paper and Printing.* In Science and Civilization in China, edited by Joseph Needham, volume 5, part 1. Cambridge: Cambridge University Press, 1985.

Twitchett, Denis. *Printing and Publishing in Medieval China.* New York: Frederick C. Beil, 1983.

——— (ed.). The Cambridge History of China. Volume 3: *Sui and T'ang China.* Cambridge: Cambridge University Press, 1979.

Vainker, S. J. *Chinese Pottery and Porcelain.* London: British Museum Press, 1991.

Watt, James C. Y., and Anne E. Wardwell. *When Ssilk was Gold: Central Asian and Chinese Ttextiles.* New York: Metropolitan Museum of Art, 1997.

Wei, Clarissa. "Why China Loves American Chain Restaurants So Much." www.eater.com, March 20, 2018.

"Why Is Western Classical Music So Popular in China?" *Wilson Quarterly*, Spring, 2012.

Wu, Dana Ying-Hui, and Jeffrey Dao-Sheng Tung. *Coming to America. The Chinese-American Experience.* Brookfield, CT: Millbrook Press, 1993.

Yung, Wing. *My Life in China and America.* New York: Holt, 1909.

Index

Gan, 107, 129
Gaokao, 169–71
Gavin Menzies, 40–41
GDP, 141, 150–51, 206, 208, 232–33
Gender equality, 152, 154
General Tso's Chicken, 191–93
Genghis Khan, 19
Golden Week, 96
Grandparents, 86–87, 89, 164, 166–67
Great Cultural Revolution, 80
Great Leap Forward, 80
Great Wall, 9, 13, 16–17, 19–20, 197
Green tea, 42, 45
Guangdong Province, 129, 148, 192
Guangzhou, 128, 148–49, 162, 164, 172, 176, 181, 197, 206, 219
Guilin, 227
Gunpowder, 54–55, 57

Han Dynasty, 14, 17, 20, 33, 47, 53–54, 56, 122
Hakka, 35, 107, 129
Hangzhou, 65, 119, 229
Han people, 14, 123–24
Health care, 80, 138
Health Effects Institute, 180
Heavenly Kingdom of Universal Peace, 26
High-speed railways, 204
Himalayas, 231
Hitler, 79, 83
Holidays, 9, 89–90
Homosexuality, 160–63
Hong Kong, 32, 45, 68, 83, 93, 97, 107, 123, 137–38, 192, 221
Hong Xiuquan, 25, 27
Hua Mulan, 31–32
Huangshan, 227
Hui, 124–25, 129
Humility, 133–34
Hunanese, 107, 129

Ian Bremmer, 231, 235
Iced tea, 45
Immigration, 71, 73, 190
Income inequality, 167
India, 12, 23, 36, 38, 41–45, 48, 53, 67, 147–48, 180, 183, 190, 232
Industrial Revolution, 49, 54
International Day Against Homophobia, 164
International students, 190
Internet, 119–20, 162, 165, 208–9, 211–12, 216–17
Islam, 185–87

Japan, 15, 20, 42, 49, 63–66, 76–77, 114, 130–34, 148, 157, 195, 209, 232
Japanese, 14–15, 42, 47–48, 60, 62–66, 76, 86, 96, 114, 130–34, 169, 173, 176
Jennifer Lee, 192
Jet Li, 61
Jingdezhen, 50–51
Jiuzhaigou, 245

Kangxi, 35, 51
KFC, 196–201
Kites, 57, 92
Koi, 63, 65–66
Kong-pao chicken, 193–94
Korea, 14–15, 23, 30, 42, 65, 109, 174, 202, 209
Koreans, 109, 125, 176, 202
Korean War, 141
Kungfu, 59–61
Kuomintang, 75, 79, 136

Lang Lang, 221
Lantern Festival, 89, 91
Lao Zi, 33, 53, 184
laws, 12, 125, 138, 158, 214, 217, 225
Lesbians, 161, 163, 165